Experiencing love, contagious joy, and Jesus at home

Pacific Press® Publishing Association
Nampa, Idaho
Oshawa, Ontario, Canada
www.pacificpress.com

Design by Dennis Ferree

Bible texts are taken from the New International Version (NIV) unless otherwise noted.
Scripture taken from the THE HOLY BIBLE, NEW INTERNATIONAL VERSION. Copyright © 1973, 1978, 1984 by International Bible Society. Used by permission of Zondervan Bible Publishers.

NEB: Scriptures quoted from NEB are from The New English Bible, copyright © 1961, 1970 by the Delegates of the Oxford University Press and the Syndics of the Cambridge University Press. Reprinted by permission.

TM: Scriptures quoted from TM or Message are from *The Message,* copyright © 1993, 1994, 1995. Used by permission of NavPress Publishing Group.

KJV: King James Version

NKJV: Scriptures quoted from NKJV are from the New King James Version, copyright © 1979, 1980, 1982, Thomas Nelson, Inc., Publishers. Used by permission. All rights reserved.

NASB: Scriptures quoted from NASB are from The New American Standard Bible, copyright © 1960, 1962, 1963, 1968, 1971, 1972, 1973, 1975, 1977, 1995 by the Lockman Foundation. Used by permission.

The Bible in Basic English

Thompson NIV: Scriptures quoted from Thompson NIV are from *The Thompson Chain Reference Bible New International Version,* copyright ©1990 by The B.B. Kirkbride Bible Company Inc.

Library of Congress Cataloging-in-Publication Data

Flowers, Karen, 1945-
Family Faith : Experiencing love, contagious joy, and Jesus at home/Karen and Ron Flowers.
p. cm.
ISBN: 0-8163-2111-6
1. Family—Religious aspects—Christianity. 2. Marriage—Religious aspects—Christianity. 3.Seventh-day Adventists—Doctrines. I. Flowers, Ron, 1944- II. Title.

BT707.7.F56 2005
248.4—dc22   2005049269

Additional copies of this book are available by calling toll free 1-800-765-6955 or visiting <http://www.adventistbookcenter.com>.

05 06 07 08 09 • 5 4 3 2 1

Also by Karen and Ron Flowers
Love Aflame

Dedicated to
Harold and Nelma Drake,
fellow pilgrims and kindred spirits
in ministry to families

Acknowledgments

Special thanks to Kathy Sowards, our administrative assistant, who worked tirelessly by long-distance phone and email to shape the manuscript when we were continents away. And to David Jarnes, our editor and friend at Pacific Press, who shortened our sentences and made us look like more polished writers than we are.

Thanks to Tim Lale, who encouraged us to undertake the project and later extended the December deadline to give us Christmas with our family.

All glory to God, who created us for relationships and bridged in Christ every chasm that separates us from heaven and from one another.

Karen and Ron
Takoma Park, Maryland

Table of Contents

Introduction

As the world moves swiftly into the third millennium after Jesus' resurrection, His response to the question of the Pharisees, "Teacher, which is the greatest commandment in the Law?" is as relevant as it was at the beginning of the first millennium. "Jesus replied: ' "Love the Lord your God with all your heart and with all your soul and with all your mind." This is the first and greatest commandment. And the second is like it: "Love your neighbor as yourself." All the Law and the Prophets hang on these two commandments' " (Matthew 22:36–40). With His answer, Jesus elevated the matter of how human beings do relationships to a spiritual plane.

First, He says, religion is about our relationship to God. His call to love God with everything that is within us is a call to respond to God's redemptive, heart-turning act in Jesus Christ. In Him, God is beckoning us in love to turn from our sinful ways and come near to Him, just as divinity and humanity shared intimate communion in the beginning. Our positive response opens the channel for God's Spirit to pour His love into our hearts. And as we trust Him, our conditional love gives way to His unconditional, agape love.

However, Jesus continued, religion is also about our relationships with one another. His command that we love our neighbors as ourselves compresses many important ideas into a few words. Human beings were created in the image of a relational God. We were created to have relationships with one another. Our desire for connectedness reflects a fundamental human need. How we do relationships with one another matters to God. *Neighbor* is an all-encompassing word meaning "the person next to us"—our parents, our marriage partners, our children, our extended family, persons living next door and in the neighborhood, fellow believers in the community of faith, people of every kindred and tongue who inhabit this global village in which we find ourselves. Always there is balance between appropriate self-care and the care of others.

Placing an additional emphasis on the importance to God of how we relate to one another, Jesus told His disciples, "A new command I give you: Love one another. As I have loved you, so you must love one another" (John 13:34; see also John 15:12; Galatians 5:14). John continued this theme in the little epistle of 1 John, making it clear that how we do relationships with one another is indeed the best litmus test of whether we have understood and responded to God's love revealed to us in Jesus. "We know," John wrote as a seasoned Christian and pastor, "that we have passed from death to life, because we love our brothers" (1 John 3:14; see also 4:7–11).

In our time, the cry of the postmodern heart mirrors this fundamental human need for connection in relationship. Harry Lee Poe, in his book *Christian Witness in a Postmodern World*, writes, "In a highly mobile society accompanied by the breakdown of the extended family as well as of the traditional family unit, relationship has become an increasingly valuable commodity because it is so difficult to obtain and maintain. The postmodern age is an anonymous age with a yearning for relationship."[1]

Poe suggests that the age of postmodernism may be Christians' finest hour because Christianity is not about an institution but about a personal God who, in Christ, has reconciled human beings to Himself and to each other. Christianity offers more than compelling doctrine. Its greatest gift to the world is God's ultimate gift, the Person Jesus Christ, who comes and makes His home with us. And even as He draws all to Himself, He closes the gaps between us—no matter what it is that divides—and restores wholeness to our broken relationships.

Helping us experience the good news for ourselves and in our families—that our joy may be full and that we may share it with others—is the purpose of this book. We may find that this focus requires us to come to Scripture with new eyes. We once took our boys to Disney World in Florida. At one exhibit there, we made our way into a large amphitheater. We were given a pair of what appeared to be sunglasses on our way in, which we were told not to put on until instructed to do so. A large screen dominated the stage, and as the lights dimmed, we were shown a lovely series of nature slides. The audience responded with *ooh*'s and *aah*'s as the wonders of God's creation were spread before us.

Then, with a picture of an apple orchard in full bloom in view, we were invited to put on the "magic" glasses we had been given. As you have probably guessed, they were 3-D—three-dimensional—glasses. As our eyes adjusted to them, suddenly, like magic, the limbs of the apple orchard spread over us. The room was abuzz with exclamations of delight, and laughter erupted everywhere as people gave in to the temptation to try to pull down a branch so they could bury their noses in the pink blossoms and imbibe the sweet fragrance. We felt like we really were in that orchard.

We pray that as you read this book you will be enticed to put on the magic glasses God has provided everyone in the person of His Son. As His call to radically different ways of doing relationship with God and each other comes into focus through the revelation of the Word made flesh and the Word preserved for us in the testimony of Scripture, may our families experience miracles of love and grace and revel in the goodness of the age to come. That will be the best sermon our neighbors will ever "hear"!

---

1. Harry Lee Poe, *Christian Witness in a Postmodern World* (Nashville, Tenn.: Abingdon Press, 2001), 27.

The Smallest Church

Here's a trivia question for you: Where is the world's largest church? Answer: It depends. The world's largest religious structure is St. Peter's Basilica in Rome, though that building doesn't usually make the list of large churches. The Cathedral Church of St. John the Divine in New York City, covering 121,000 square feet (the equivalent of two National Football League fields), crowns many lists. But others would claim the top spot for the Basilica of Our Lady of Peace in Yamoussoukro, Cote d'Ivoire, with its seating capacity of eighteen thousand.

What about the smallest church? Many miniature church edifices claim to be the smallest, but if floor dimensions are the primary criteria, a diminutive, white, wood-frame chapel raising its steeple near Oneida, New York, holds the title. The Internet Web site "Tiny Churches" says, "Oneida, New York: 3.5 × 6 feet. . . . Fits a minister, bride and groom."[1]

Such trivia typically lead us to identify "church" as a building. But think again. What does "church" really mean?

It's not about the building

The contemporary English word "church" has its roots in the Greek *kyriakos,* which means "belonging to the Lord" or simply "the Lord's." Used to refer to "the Lord's table" (1 Corinthians 10:21) and "the Lord's Day" (Revelation 1:10), *kyriakos* also became the nomenclature in the second and third centuries for the house of worship—the building too was "the Lord's."

The New Testament Greek word that translators render in English as "church" is *ekklēsia* (from a Greek word meaning "called out"). We can see *ekklēsia* in ecclesiastic and ecclesiastical. The French and Spanish words for "church," *église* and *iglesia,* respectively, are directly traceable to the original *ekklēsia.* However, the writers of the Bible did not have church buildings in mind when they used the term *ekklēsia.* Rather, they used this term to refer to the community of faith, the assembly of those who have been "called out." The essence of the New Testament concept of church, then, is not architectural, but relational. The church is the community of believers.

A close-knit community is exactly what Jesus designed His church to be. Again and again He spoke of relationships between church members as characterized by self-giving love. Summing up the law of God in Matthew 22:37–40, Jesus pointed out that it all boils down to love extended in two directions: First, " ' "Love the Lord your God with all your heart and with all your soul and with all your mind" ' " (verse 37). Then, " ' "Love your neighbor as yourself" ' " (verse 39). Thus Jesus placed human relationships on a moral plane comparable to our relationship with God. Loving relationships are at the core of God's revealed will: " 'All the Law and the Prophets hang on these two commandments' " (verse 40).

The Gospel of John tells us that Christ specifically charged His followers to love one another: " 'A new command I give you: Love one another. As I have loved you, so you must love one another. By this all men will know that you are my disciples, if you love one another' " (John 13:34, 35). Later, the apostles echoed Jesus' call:

> Dear friends, let us love one another, for love comes from God. . . . This is love: not that we loved God, but that he loved us and sent his Son as an atoning sacrifice for our sins. Dear friends, since God so loved us, we also ought to love one another. . . .
>
> And he has given us this command: Whoever loves God must also love his brother (1 John 4:7–11, 21).

It is to this fellowship of love that the apostles beckon us: "We proclaim to you what we have seen and heard, so that you also may have fellowship with us. And our fellowship is with the Father and with his Son, Jesus Christ" (1 John 1:3). The intimacy of this fellowship is opened to our imaginations in a brief passage in Acts 2:42–47—a description that would take on flesh and blood in the stories of life in the early church that Luke and the apostle Paul recorded for posterity. It is an extraordinary experience of community and togetherness they called *koinōnia* (Acts 2:42), one of the richest words in the New Testament (see other examples in 1 Corinthians 1:9; Galatians 2:9; Philippians 1:5; 1 John 1:3).

They "had everything in common" (Acts 2:44)—spiritually, socially, and materially. They were distinct individuals with a variety of ideas and gifts, yet they moved as one organism with a passion for Jesus Christ and for sharing the good news that in Him, God's favor once again rested upon humankind. These verses at the end of Acts 2 are, as G. Campbell Morgan once put it, the "continuing result," the "enlarging result," the "immediate result" of individuals being convinced and convicted when the Spirit-filled preacher Peter lifted up the crucified Jesus as Lord and Christ.[2] The picture is one that still inspires awe.

A favorite devotional experience Ron and I share is an ongoing search for what we have come to call the "one-anothering" texts—New Testament passages in which the words "one another" appear. When we share our collection with others, many are surprised at the number and comprehensiveness of the references. The texts practically preach themselves. We often hear comments like: "We don't spend enough time on these subjects." "We'd be a different people if we did this!" "What a church God intends for us to be!"

The starter list that follows creates an amazing collage of the kinds of interpersonal relationships that God wants to characterize this Christian fellowship called "church":

New Testament "One Anothers"
- Love one another (1 Thessalonians 3:12)
- Accept one another, just as Christ accepted you (Romans 15:7)
- Greet one another (2 Corinthians 13:12)

- Have the same care for one another (1 Corinthians 11:33)
- Submit to one another (Ephesians 5:21)
- Bear with one another in love (Ephesians 4:2)
- Confess your sins to one another (James 5:16)
- Forgive one another (Ephesians 4:32)
- Build one another (Ephesians 4:29)
- Teach and admonish one another in all wisdom (Colossians 3:16)
- Exhort one another (Hebrews 10:25)
- Instruct one another (Romans 15:14)
- Speak to one another in psalms, hymns, and spiritual songs, always giving thanks (Ephesians 5:19, 20)
- Comfort one another (1 Thessalonians 4:18)
- Serve one another in love (Galatians 5:13)
- Bear one another's burdens (Colossians 3:13)
- Offer hospitality to one another without grumbling (1 Peter 4:9)
- Be kind to one another (1 Thessalonians 5:15)
- Pray for one another (James 5:16)
- Do not judge one another (Romans 14:13)
- Do not speak evil of one another (James 4:11)
- Do not murmur against one another (James 5:9)
- Do not bite and devour one another (Galatians 5:15)
- Do not provoke and envy each other (Galatians 5:26)
- Do not lie to one another (Colossians 3:9)

A family template

The primary template Jesus employed to design His new community called "church" was that of a household, a family. The various Bible writers, as they were moved by the Holy Spirit, also had family in mind as they shaped the fellowship of believers by their preaching and writing. Followers of Jesus are "members of God's household" (Ephesians 2:19). Believers are children of God (1 Corinthians 4:14), brothers and sisters in Christ (1 Timothy 5:1, 2). Bible writers borrowed from family life the metaphors of birth (John 3:4–8; 1 Peter 1:23; 1 John 5:1) and the birthing process (Galatians 4:19), along with that of adoption (Galatians 4:5; Ephesians 1:5) to explain the process by which people become part of the redeemed community of Christ. Comparisons with everyday family responsibilities, such as providing for the needs of growing children, offer a well-understood shorthand for Christian growth (Hebrews 5:12–14; 1 Corinthians 13:11). Older members in the church are to be fathers and mothers to the generations that follow them (1 Timothy 5:1, 2). And the crowning family motifs open windows on God Himself as patient and loving Father (Matthew 5:16, 45, 48; John 20:17; 2 Corinthians 6:18) and Jesus as beloved Bridegroom and Husband, uniting Himself for eternity with the church, His cherished bride (Isaiah 54:5; 62:5; Hosea 3:1; Revelation 19:6–10).

Some think this use of family language to speak of the church indicates a shift in God's mind-set. They say that in the past, He selected a household—Abraham and his line—to be His agents on earth, and He confirmed His covenant with them by saying "you will be a blessing . . . and all peoples on earth will be blessed through you" (Genesis 12:2, 3). But now, they continue, God has invested in a new plan. This line of thinking suggests that sin has so marred marriage, the covenant family has become so problematic and self-centered, and the process of faith transmission between generations has become so unreliable, that God has replaced families with the church. However, as we shall see, the Bible nowhere indicates that God has replaced families as His primary setting for making disciples, for discipling and nurturing believers and disseminating truth. Instead, God has enfolded families within the bosom of a larger family, the church, to strengthen and equip them for this all-important, life-affirming responsibility.

Certain things Jesus said do deserve special attention because people have interpreted them as indicating that He placed little value on kinship relations. Once, His mother and brothers came looking for Him.

"Who are my mother and my brothers?" he asked.

Then he looked at those seated in a circle around him and said, "Here are my mother and my brothers! Whoever does God's will is my brother and sister and mother" (Mark 3:32–35).

On the surface it might seem that here Jesus was, at the very least, ignoring His family, choosing to be with His disciples instead.

Careful study of this and other so-called "difficult sayings" along this line (cp. Luke 9:59–62; 11:27, 28; 14:26; 18:29, 30; 20:34–36; John 2:4), however, yields other interpretations that do not diminish the importance of family ties. Take, for example, Matthew 10:34–36, where Jesus says,

> "I did not come to bring peace, but a sword. For I have come to turn
>   " 'a man against his father,
>   a daughter against her mother,
>   a daughter-in-law against her mother-in-law—
>   a man's enemies will be the members of his own
>   household' " (Matthew 10:34–36).

There is good evidence that Jesus was not expressing antifamily sentiment in this saying. The original readers of the book of Matthew would have immediately recognized that He was referencing a well-known and oft-repeated truism of the day that spoke of the coming of the Messiah. William Barclay explains, "The Jews believed that one of the features of the Day of the Lord, the day when God would break into history, would be the division of families. The Rabbis said: 'In the period when the Son of David shall come, a daughter will rise up against her mother, a daughter-in-law against her mother-in-law.' 'The son despises his father, the daughter rebels against the mother, the daughter-in-law against her mother-in-law, and the man's enemies are they of his own household.' It is as if Jesus said, 'The end you have always been waiting for has come; and the intervention of God in history is splitting homes and groups and families into two.' "[3]

So, Jesus was using this saying so familiar to His hearers to reveal that He Himself is the fulfillment of that long-awaited Day of the Lord.

After reviewing the various statements that at first appear hard to understand, David Garland concluded that Jesus was not in any way minimizing the value He placed on family relationships. He didn't think of the family as a petty concern or an impediment to commitment to God. Far from undercutting the importance of the nurture, support, and strength provided by families, Jesus instead was making a point about the elitist attitudes of those who trusted implicitly in their bloodlines and biological kinship for salvation. His point, says Garland, was that "intimate, satisfying family relationships, as valuable as they may be, must not be allowed to substitute for an intimate relationship with Abba."[4] Our Lord affirmed family loyalties, even as He put them into perspective against our highest loyalty, which we owe to God alone. Jesus opened the way for service to God not only within the structure of the biological family but also in the wider circle of the church, the family of God.

Family and church—inseparable and interdependent

The dust had barely settled behind the moving van when we began to acquaint ourselves with the people in our newly assigned congregations. Our visits exposed trouble brewing in many of the families. As the situation took clearer shape before our eyes, we were staggered by the reality facing us. We were a young pastoral couple, hardly prepared in our ministerial training for the open hostility, marital infidelity, and parent-adolescent conflict—the general breakdown of marriage and family relationships that was evidenced, it seemed, at every turn.

Afraid to admit the extent of the crises facing us lest the presence of such problems in the congregations to whom we ministered reflect on our competence, we cautiously approached a few trusted ministry colleagues. We posed hypothetical scenarios and asked what they would do in the unlikely event that they faced them. "Don't worry about it," they said in their effort to comfort us. "Families will be families, and families have problems. Stay focused. Remember, your primary responsibility is not to mess with family problems. Stick with the work of the church. With any luck, the people will become so involved that they'll forget their troubles at home."

They meant well. However, the conviction was growing upon us that we could make no artificial distinction between family and church or between a ministry to families and the mission of the church. Families—with all their needs, strengths, and challenges—

collectively make up the church. The church is a household of households, a family of families. At the same time, each family unit is itself a small church within the larger body of Christ. And the strength of each relates directly to the strength of the other.

The biblical witness is that home and church are indeed inseparable. They have been intertwined from the earliest days. The relational vocabulary of the smaller community of the family was employed both to describe and to shape life within the larger community of the church.

Often, churches met in the homes of the members. In his letter to Philemon, Paul sent greetings to Philemon, to his wife Apphia, to their son Archippus, "and to the church that meets in your home" (Philemon 1, 2). Mary, mother of John Mark and sister of Barnabas, opened her home to the oft-beleaguered believers. It was to her home that Peter headed immediately after he was miraculously released from prison, knowing he would find fellow believers there (Acts 12:11–17). The believers first experienced joyous fellowship in household settings as they "broke bread in their homes and ate together with glad and sincere hearts" (Acts 2:46).

Just as today, the families and households of New Testament times existed in a wide variety of forms—singles, married couples, parent(s) with children, families without children, grandparents raising their grandchildren, Christians married to non-Christians, extended family networks living together and apart. Each was a small faith-center, seeking to disciple its own members and contributing to the larger faith-center, the church. The spiritual gifts Timothy brought to his ministry in the church, for example, were cultivated at home by his mother, Eunice, and grandmother, Lois (2 Timothy 1:5). Home-based Bible study can be powerful indeed in the life of the church. Scripture specifically notes that when Priscilla and Aquila heard the great preacher Apollos but discerned that he had not yet received the full light of the gospel, "they invited him to their home and explained to him the way of God more adequately" (Acts 18:26).

Heart of the church

Many times those early missionaries presented the gospel to extended families, who came together to listen and learn. Often whole family groups responded. The roll call of such households is impressive: the Jewish nobleman's household (John 4:46–53), Cornelius's household with relatives and friends (Acts 10:2, 24, 44–48), Lydia's household (Acts 16:11–15), the entire households of the synagogue ruler Crispus (Acts 18:8), of Aristobulus (Romans 16:10), Onesiphorus (2 Timothy 4:19), and Stephanas, members of whose household were referred to as the first converts in Achaia (1 Corinthians 16:15). Traditionally, Stephanas has been thought to be the Philippian jailer whose "whole family was filled with joy, because they had come to believe in God" (Acts 16:31–34, Thompson NIV).

"Greet those in the household of Narcissus who are in the Lord," wrote Paul (Romans 16:11). Where family members confess faith in Christ together, such a household "in the Lord" is essentially a microcosm of the larger body of Christ, a minichurch within a church. Rather than being replaced by the community of faith, Christian believers who are joined by earthly family ties become also brothers and sisters in Christ, with Christ as their Elder Brother and God their heavenly Father.

As the experience of being family on earth takes on new dimensions for Christian families, the Holy Spirit binds these "household churches" together into a new fellowship. United in Christ, the church becomes far more than the sum of the households. Together they become a living, vibrant body, each family vital to the strength and encouragement of the others and to the health of the church as a whole. It is true that the church can be no stronger than the families that comprise it. But it is also true that, when enfolded into such a community, weak households can receive an experience in grace that will create their best chance of laying hold of its transforming power. While the church draws upon the ties that bind individual family members together, the power of the gospel that brings unity out of diversity in the church also infuses individual family circles with a new love not of human origin, a love that transforms family relationships, enriching and strengthening all within its reach.

Yes, confirms Ellen White, "every family is a church."[5] Elsewhere she said, "Out of the heart are 'the issues of life' (Proverbs 4:23); and the heart of the community, of the church, and of the nation is the household. The well-being of society, the success of the church, the prosperity of the nation, depend upon home influences."[6]

Anna Graham literally was the heart of the Londonderry Seventh-day Adventist Church in Northern Ireland for a critical period in its history. Long years of political strife and contention between Christian groups have left many in Derry jaded toward religion. New members are hard to come by. In the latter part of the 1990s, the Seventh-day Adventist church in that city was on the brink of extinction. Most of the tiny membership had died or moved or simply didn't attend. For two years, Anna came to church alone, single-handedly keeping the church alive.

Responsible for multiple churches, pastors assigned to Derry were often engaged elsewhere. "Sometimes a pastor from Belfast would come," she told us. "I and whoever came to preach sat together, and then maybe he would give a short talk.

"There were many weeks when I sat by myself and prayed and studied the Sabbath School lesson," she remembers. "No one else came. I used to sit and play the organ—out of my head, with one hand—and sing to pass the time. Then I would go home." Home was twelve miles away, and three of those miles she walked to get the bus.

Then one Sabbath, her prayer for others to join her was answered. A university student came to church. The tide turned. One by one, others came. "The church is growing now," she told us in a recent trans-Atlantic phone call. She continues to be a source of inspiration there. Hers is a testimony to what each member, each household means to the health and well-being of the larger body.

Heart health is a vital concern in society at large these days. In the church too, we will do well to devote attention to keeping the "heart" healthy. What can we do to reduce the risk factors for heart disease, or worse, heart failure? What will make for strong hearts? If we would grow and maintain healthy churches, we must look to strengthen this smallest foundational unit within the body of Christ.

1. "Tiny Churches" Web site: <www.roadsideamerica.com/set/church.html>.

2. G. Campbell Morgan, *The Birth of the Church: An Exposition of the Second Chapter of Acts* (Old Tappan, N.J.: Fleming H. Revell, 1968), 150.

3. William Barclay, *The Gospel of Matthew,* revised edition (Philadelphia: The Westminster Press, 1975), 1:393.

4. David E. Garland, "A Biblical Foundation for Family Ministry," Diana S. Garland and Diane L. Pancoast, eds., *The Church's Ministry with Families* (Dallas: Word Publishing, 1990), 32.

5. Ellen G. White, *Child Guidance* (Hagerstown, Md.: Review and Herald, 1954), 549.

6. Ellen G. White, *The Ministry of Healing* (Nampa, Idaho: Pacific Press®, 1942), 349, emphasis supplied.

CHAPTER

An Owner's Manual for Family Living

The other day while Ron had his new world phone and all of its accompanying paraphernalia spread out, our son Jon happened in on him. Ron was struggling to work out the phone's high-tech features. He pressed buttons that had worked on his old phone; now they didn't give the anticipated results. Time after time, he passed the phone to Jon for help. Eventually, Jon looked at him and said earnestly, "Dad, this phone is complicated. I've never seen one like it. You might just have to take time to read the instructions."

Jon was right. You can't hope to maximize the valuable features of any complex device without studying the manufacturer's instructions. The same is true for families. Living together intimately in two-parent families, single-parent families, or stepfamilies—or in whatever form a family takes—is no less demanding than operating the most intricate of electronic gear. Yet human beings often embark on the responsibilities of marriage and parenting with nothing but past experience—for better or worse—to guide their behavior. Where can families turn for a reliable, user-friendly owner's manual for family living?

Truth in an ancient text

For long ages, countless people have turned for guidance to the anthology of writings—the sacred library—that we call the Bible. This volume is sacred not because it is old and has been revered throughout time but because it is more than *a* book. It is *the* Book about God and His relationship with humankind. As Eugene Peterson observes in his "Introduction to the New Testament" in *The Message* translation, "the early Christians, whose lives were being changed and shaped by what they were reading, arrived at the conviction that . . . God's Holy Spirit was behind and in it all. . . . They were bold to call what had been written 'God's Word,' and trusted their lives to it. They accepted its authority over their lives. Most of its readers since have been similarly convinced."[1] Herein God has revealed the divine vision for humankind in relationship to Himself and to one another. "Your word is a lamp to my feet and a light for my path," wrote the psalmist in a beautiful hymn (Psalm 119:105).

Nature too holds truth within its bosom—truth to be discovered, enjoyed, and contemplated about Creator-God, His wondrous creation, and the principles that govern its inner workings. "The heavens declare the glory of God; the skies proclaim the work of his hands" says another of the psalmist's hymns (Psalm 19:1). This secondary revelation, which includes both the natural and social sciences, is an important source of information about human beings and what makes them tick. However, we interpret it safely only in harmony with the biblical worldview.

Most people pay little attention to Scripture as a source of guidance for living together in family and community. Perhaps social realities have rendered some pastors silent regarding the application of scriptural teaching to family living. Research among married Christians in the United States, for example, indicates that 35 percent have experienced a divorce.[2] Many pastors, sensitive to the presence of divorcees in their congregations, have expressed hesitancy to preach about marriage lest they contribute to their pain.

Many cultural practices, such as those regarding sexuality, are at odds with Scripture. In Western societies, many people no longer consider sex outside of marriage to be a moral issue. Rather, the primary concerns are to prevent unwanted pregnancy and to avoid sexually transmitted infections—most specifically, the dread HIV/AIDS virus. Increasingly, people consider cohabitation an acceptable alternative to marriage. Between 1960 and 2002, the number of unmarried couples living together in the United States increased by 1,100 percent.[3]

The Bible's principles are broad enough to accommodate a wide range of cultural as well as individual couple differences. However, these principles also set boundaries on human behavior, marking what God, as Creator, says is good or harmful to His beloved creation, what is clearly inside or outside His divine design for human relationships. Certainly, the Bible is clear that in God's plan, sexual relations belong within the covenant of marriage, a lifelong commitment solemnized before both God and community.

The church's dealings with individuals and families have not always been ideal. Thus, many doubt that the church—and the Bible it claims to embrace—can be trustworthy sources of help on contemporary issues. Some merely write the Bible off as antiquated and irrelevant. Others misunderstand its teachings as standing in the way of human progress. Either way, many people no longer consider it a source of dynamic principles on living in relationship.

Sadly, we Christians have not always been faithful to the Bible. By word and action we have distorted its teachings and the face of the God behind its principles. It remains for us now to reach out to those who have been hurt by so-called believers who have acted in ways incompatible with the character of Christ's caring ministry and the principles of His kingdom. We must commit ourselves anew to the winsome unfolding of Scripture as present truth that can help individuals and families deal with issues of very real and contemporary concern. As we open the Bible to contemporary society, many will be drawn to its life-affirming principles and experience its power in their families as did the men and women who encountered the same Book and the God of the Book for the first time some two thousand years ago.

Ancient mariners used the stars as reference points for navigation. The Southern Cross helped them find the South Pole. In the north, they looked to the Big Dipper to point them to Polaris—the North Star. By today's standards, their navigational methods were primitive. Now even cars sport GPSs—global-positioning systems that rely on an array of satellites stationed above the earth. It would seem the stars are outdated when it comes to finding one's way. That is, it seems so until we discover that each global-positioning satellite uses a "star tracker" instrument to maintain its orientation in space. The satellites themselves rely on the stars as reference points—stars have not outlived this purpose after all!

So too with God's Word. There is truth for today in this ancient text. Across time, as social, political, economic, and technological change have molded family relationships and the plethora of complex issues confronting them, the Bible has proven itself equal to the challenge. The stars of principle found within its pages provide the ideals toward which all Christians stretch, even as we come together in the church to make meaning of these principles in various time frames and cultural settings.

He who has eyes, let him see

A naturalist at a weekend retreat once gave each member of our family a portrait-sized mirror and sent us for a walk in the woods. Our assignment: Hold the mirrors face up at waist level in front of us, look into them as we walked through the trees, and talk to each other about what we saw. The view was breathtaking! We felt as though we were seeing the world from a whole new vantage point, as you might imagine it looks to a squirrel or monkey. We seemed to be right in the very treetops, with blue sky and sunshine outlining a leaf in blue and gold here and illuminating a strange anomaly in bark there. One minute the wind drew the branches together into a grand archway; the next, a dazzling expanse of sky opened overhead. It was an unforgettable way of looking at the world around us, most of which we wouldn't have noticed without the mirrors.

Accustomed as we are to viewing the Word of God with theological glasses, we may miss its relational themes. But we can see the familiar in Scripture with new eyes when we come to it intentionally attuned to its relational themes. When we think "family" as we study, the Bible will open to us afresh as a veritable textbook on the principles that govern Christian relationships in general and family relationships in particular. Many and varied are the means God uses to convey His practical lessons on family living.

Relational commandments. The Bible has a few direct commands that speak precisely to family relationships: " 'Honor your father and your mother' " (Exodus 20:12). " 'You shall not commit adultery' " (Exodus 20:14). "Submit to one another out of reverence for Christ. Wives, submit to your husbands as to the Lord. . . . Husbands, love your wives, just as Christ loved the church and gave himself up for her" (Ephesians 5:21, 22, 25). Other general relational directives apply to relationships in the home as well: " 'Do to others what you would have them do to you' " (Matthew 7:12). " 'Love one another' " (John 13:34). "Be kind and compassionate to one another, forgiving each other, just as in Christ God forgave you" (Ephesians 4:32).

Relational principles. The Bible also unmasks natural laws and relational principles common to human interaction across time and culture. Proverbs has the largest collection of these. Such passages offer insight into the psychological principles implanted within men and women by the Creator that anticipate a universal human response: "An anxious heart weighs a man down, but a kind word cheers him up" (Proverbs 12:25). "A gentle answer turns away wrath, but a harsh word stirs up anger" (Proverbs 15:1). "Gossip separates close friends" (Proverbs 16:28).

Family narratives. The Bible contains both parables about families, like the waiting father (Luke 15:11–32) and the stories of real families, like Abraham and Sarah (Genesis 12:1–25:10), Isaac, Rebekah, Jacob, and Esau (Genesis 27), Naomi, Ruth, and Boaz (Ruth 1–4), and Elkanah, Hannah, and Samuel (1 Samuel 1–3). These stories and parables instruct, encourage, and correct us (Romans 15:4; 2 Timothy 3:16). They open a window of understanding on the inner workings of family systems. Readers everywhere find themselves in them. We take comfort in the knowledge that we are not alone in temptation and trial, in struggle and setback. And because they portray God as longsuffering and patient with those who have gone before, we take heart that He will be so with us.

In addition, through the Scripture's honesty in revealing the weaknesses and mistakes of God's people of old, we can discern more clearly the pitfalls that lie before us and better avoid them. And as we watch in wonder the miracles of grace worked out in the lives of those who unclasped their hands to receive God's gracious guidance and correction, we find hope for our families. In their victories, we gain courage to take steps toward the change needed in our own lives.

Family metaphors. The Bible uses metaphors of family to describe God's relationship with His people. These family metaphors enlighten our understanding of how He wants us to live together—how to relate to one another. Scripture pictures God as a *bridegroom* and *husband* to His people (Isaiah 54:5; 62:5; Jeremiah 3:14; 31:32; 2 Corinthians 11:2; Revelation 21:2, 9) and as a *father* to them (2 Samuel 7:14; Jeremiah 31:9; Matthew 6:9; Luke 23:34; Ephesians 3:14; Revelation 1:6). Several verses also describe God as nurturing and caring for His own like a *mother* (Deuteronomy 32:11; Isaiah 49:15; 66:12ff; Hosea 11:1–4; Matthew 23:37). By pondering these images of God as marriage partner and parent, we learn more about our responsibilities and the kind of relationships God wants for us. As we stretch toward these divine ideals in our homes, family members see God more clearly as a God of love.

Love poetry. From the dawn of time, the attraction of male and female to each other has been cause for poetry and song. Adam burst into ecstatic poetic verse as he came out of his slumber and found himself in the presence of a beautiful companion, handcrafted as his perfect soul mate by the Creator Himself. "This is now bone of my bones and flesh of my flesh; she shall be called 'woman,' for she was taken out of man" (Genesis 2:23).

The Song of Solomon is a whole Bible book devoted to unfolding the mysteries of human bonding and the delights of married love. This special piece of divinely inspired Hebrew poetry contains some of Scripture's best insights on how we form and maintain intimate relationships. In the Song of Solomon, the God who created human sexuality and declared it to be very good (Genesis 1:31) preserves the story of Solomon and Shulamith as a celebration of marriage and the most intimate expression of love entrusted to humankind.

Jesus' affirmation of families. Jesus reaffirmed His original intent for marriage by citing the Genesis account of its creation (Matthew 19:5; cp. Genesis 2:24). By His presence and ministry at the wedding reception in Cana, He again upheld the marriage institution (John 2:1–12).[4] In the transformation of water to wine, Jesus left us a sign of His power to redeem not only a social situation for one embarrassed family but also to redeem husband-wife relationships for all time. The master of the feast declared the divine elixir Jesus created to be the best wine he had ever tasted. Similarly, Jesus wants our marriages to be the best ever created. Elsewhere, He elevated marriage to an even loftier plane as He likened His love for His church to the passionate love of a bridegroom for his bride (Matthew 9:15; Mark 2:19, 20; cp. John 3:29; Revelation 19:9).

Jesus often talked of children and the love ties that bind them to their parents. During His sojourn on earth, He was always ready to listen to children and their oft-weary parents, drawing them close to Himself, soothing them with His touch and tender words of solace and blessing. His parenting illustrations and stories (see Matthew 7:9–11; Luke 15:11–32) are as poignant today as when He spoke them. He gave His life for children as well as for adults.[5]

Lessons from church. As we have seen, family is a major source of metaphors in Scripture for teaching us how God would have us to relate to each other in the church. Conversely, believers bring to their homes their experience in the wider family of God. Good relational experiences in the church inspire deeper commitment to the family values that are the warp and woof of the kingdom of God. The circle of learning is thus complete: family informing church, and church informing family—each a practical lesson to the other in God's relational design.

A view from the heights

As Ron and I flew into Belem, Brazil, some years ago, we caught our first glimpse of the Amazon. This colossus of rivers, 150 miles wide and 300 feet deep at its mouth, begins as a myriad of small streams cascading down the eastern slopes of the Andes Mountains in Peru, more than four thousand miles from the river's mouth. Along the way, these tiny rivulets swell into more than a thousand rivers that, in turn, merge to create one mighty flow to the sea. So Scripture's lessons on family come together in an extraordinary stream of revelation, creating a body of teachings rich and full.

Scripture also offers another very important "view from the heights." It establishes God's perspective on a set of essential questions without which human beings will never be able to make sense of the world—questions like "Who am I?" "Where did I come from?" "What is wrong here?" and "What is the solution?" Scholars call people's answers to these important questions their "worldview." Familiarity with the biblical worldview not only helps us make sense of reality as we experience it, it is also foundational to understanding the teachings of the Bible, including its teachings about families.

Primary elements in the Christian worldview are an understanding of *creation, sin,* and *redemption.*

In the first chapters, a perfect *creation* occupies the foreground, with details of the making of male and female in the image of God and the formation of the first family (Genesis 1:26–2:25). With the temptation and fall of humankind, we get a glimpse of *sin,* its nature, and its already far-reaching, devastating effects on creation, including marriage and the family (Genesis 3:1–24). *Redemption* is present from the beginning in the God who searches for His beloved children while they were yet sinners, covers their nakedness, and promises the eradication of sin in His own victory over the evil one (Genesis 3:15). During the march of history toward Calvary, God's Spirit lifts the mist that sin casts over the landscape, exposing the great controversy between Christ and Satan and revealing more and more particulars of God's worldview. The redemptive activity of Christ makes everything plain for all who have eyes to see.

The biblical worldview regarding sin provides an important aid to understanding human nature and making sense of relationships as they play out in real life. For example, we see aspects of human nature and human relational processes that continue to bear witness to the Creator's original design. At the same time, the ravages of sin dim our comprehension and confuse the picture of reality that we derive from observation of the natural world alone.

For example, social scientists who observe the loving bonds present between most mothers and their babies from birth might conclude that the human heart is by nature loving and committed to the care and nurture of its children. Scripture confirms that this attachment between mother and child does indeed bear witness to the Creator's original design (Deuteronomy 1:31; Isaiah 49:15; Matthew 7:9–11). However, sin is also evident in human relationships—a present, willful force that manifests itself in human nature as a bent toward selfishness and conditional love. These distortions of God's original design will ultimately govern human relationships apart from a conscious decision to die to sin and rise to a new and radically different life in Christ.

Christians do well to study the social sciences as a venture into understanding the revelation of God's "second book" of nature and to share with the world the myriad ways science corroborates relational truths first revealed by God Himself. But only when lessons from the natural world are compatible with the biblical worldview can we safely incorporate them into what we discern to be the body of "God's truth."

We have a friend in Australia who loves to remind us that Sydney harbor is "the finest harbor in the world." As proof, he once took us up the Sydney Tower to a vantage point 750 feet above the city. Close in was the Harbour Bridge and the world-renowned opera house, with its graceful, lotus-blossom lines. In the distant west, the Blue Mountains were silhouetted in the purple mist of the sunset. To the north and south, the coastline seemed to unwind like a ball of yarn beyond our view. Our friend stood there with us on the observation deck, enjoying our gasps as we struggled to take in the breathtaking beauty of the awesome harbor that wrapped around us. There's nothing like a view from the heights to put the landscape in perspective.

Only Scripture, with its reference point in eternity, can fully provide a view from the heights that opens for us an amazing array of insights into God's design for the family. Such a view also brings into clear focus the multiplied losses for the institutions of marriage and family that sin has produced. We see ourselves in this panorama. We see why we long for love and intimacy, as well as why we find it hard to live out God's ideals in the family circle. Most importantly, we find hope and help in the person of One who has made us family in the Beloved. It's a view we can't afford to miss.

---

1. Eugene Peterson, *The Message: The Bible in Contemporary Language* (Colorado Springs: NavPress, 2002), 1319.

2. "Born Again Christians Just As Likely to Divorce As Are Non-Christians" The Barna Update, online (September 8, 2004). Retrieved December 7, 2004, from <http://www.barna.org/FlexPage.aspx?Page=BarnaUpdateNarrow&BarnaUpdateI D=170.html>.

3. The National Marriage Project, *The State of Our Unions* (New Brunswick: Rutgers, The State University of New Jersey, 2004), 20.

4. Ellen G. White, *The Ministry of Healing* (Nampa, Idaho: Pacific Press®, 1942), 356.

5. Ellen G. White, *The Adventist Home* (Hagerstown, Md.: Review and Herald, 1952), 279.

Becoming Us

Last night Ron and I looked at our wedding album. If you'd been looking over our shoulders, you would have smiled at the sunburned, lanky farm boy, grinning from ear to ear as if he had just harvested the bumper crop of his life, and the small-town girl with freckles and big, brown eyes. The vows we made to each other that day promised the moon. But we had precious little idea what married life was really all about.

In our day, little was written or said about preparation for marriage. In fairness to the pastor who married us, he tried. We spent a session with him in which he brought out a game with questions designed to open a conversation about significant marital issues. Today, we affirm him as way ahead of his time, doing his best to prepare us for what lay ahead. Then, we didn't think it was necessary. Oh, we knew that the rate of divorces was increasing. But we were over twenty, we were in love, and we were Christians. Surely, these were credentials enough to prepare us for marriage. If we had known how stacked the odds were against us (only about 5 percent of all couples as different in temperament and personality traits as we are stay together), we might have thought twice about things.

Reality set in fast. We both had distinct expectations about how things should be done. Karen grew up in a family in which her dad did a lot of cooking, and he was good at it. He recognized his wife's abilities in other areas. He also had a strong commitment to mutuality in marriage, and he lived out his values every day as he carried his share of the domestic duties. The family routines were dependable, but not rigid. Meal times, for instance, were flexible enough to accommodate the family's variable daily schedules. Karen came to marriage with the assumption that all couples sized up what each did well and distributed responsibilities accordingly, just as her dad and mom had done.

In Ron's family, a very different scenario was in place. His mother cared for everything related to food, clothing, and other aspects of the domestic scene. She was in charge inside the house and outside to the perimeter of her tidy flowerbeds. Ron's dad took responsibility for the farm. If it was 6:00 A.M., or 12:00 noon, or 6:00 P.M., it was mealtime—you could set your watch by it. Ron hardly opened the refrigerator. When he was hungry, he would hang around the kitchen. His mother would ask him what he wanted, and then she'd fix it.

So Karen and Ron returned from their honeymoon. The clock struck twelve o'clock noon in their little seminary apartment. Ron is puzzled when Karen makes no move to put down her studies and fix lunch. Perhaps her watch is slow. Finally, Ron runs out of patience and says, "It's twelve o'clock."

"Hey, thanks for the time check," she replies. A few not-so-subtle hints later, however, Ron is sure she's gotten the message: He's hungry and expects her to fix food! Instead, however, she flashes a smile in his direction and says matter-of-factly, "Oh, sorry, Honey. I have to finish this paper before class. I don't have time to eat lunch. But if you're hungry, there's lots of food in the fridge!" Ron feels a twinge of irritation, but he brushes it aside.

Most couples in the flush of the honeymoon brush a lot of things aside. They want nothing to burst the bubble of romance. But as powerful a force as romance is, it eventually begins to ebb as the irritations pile up. Differences start to chafe. People start to keep score. They grow weary of pasting on a grin in public. Out of the public eye, they know they're not the perfect couple everyone thinks they are.

The Story of Us

We once caught the movie *The Story of Us* on an overnight flight, and it left a deep impression. As the film title comes up, even the graphics are cleverly symbolic. The letters "U" and "S" drift back and forth across the screen. Sometimes they merge; sometimes they pass like express trains running on parallel tracks in opposite directions; sometimes they pause to linger briefly side by side—like so many partners in marriage.

Ben opens the story with a soliloquy about how he'd always wanted to marry Katie and be like those couples who remained married for fifty or sixty years—the ones who were so close and loving that when one died, the other died too, of a broken heart. Katie follows with her own monologue. She tells of reading a book called *Harold and the Purple Crayon.* It is about a boy who colors outside the lines and draws the world as he wants it to be. Well, Ben has turned out to be "her Harold." While his easy-going, spontaneous way is probably what drew her to him in the first place, she has grown weary of always having to be the responsible one in the marriage. She is tired of always having to make sure the lunches are packed, and the kids get to their dentist appointments, and on and on, while her partner lives in a fun fantasy world, as though none of this matters.

After a while, all communication revolves around their differentness:

"You never listen."

"You can't let go of anything."

"So I haven't done anything right for fifteen years?"

"Why does everything have to be programmed? Can't you ever do anything spontaneously? What happened to the fun girl I married?"

"She died, and you killed her!"

Eventually, their smiles and even their touches are just a front they keep up for the children.

Katie and Ben separate while their kids are at summer camp. Loneliness tempts them to try to reconcile; however, it doesn't work, so they make the decision to divorce. But how will they tell the kids? Over a nice meal might be good. But where—at a favorite restaurant or at home? They conclude that it'll be best to make the announcement at home. It'll be easier than in public. So they wait nervously for the bus bringing their kids back from camp. . . .

Oneness from the Creator's hand

Marriage is one of two divinely created institutions to come with our first parents out of Eden. "Twin institutions for the glory of God in the benefit of humanity," they have been called.[1] But they are melded together by more than simply a common origin. The Sabbath is a memorial to the goodness of our Creator-God and His perfect creation, including the institutions of marriage and family. It's also an every-seventh-day reminder of the spiritual rest that is ours in Christ. In Him we are reconciled to God, and earth and heaven are again restored to a state of "oneness" as in the beginning.

Christian marriage also stands as a testimony to oneness restored. Marriage in Eden was an experience of "one-flesh" unity; of openness and vulnerability born of complete trust; of physical, emotional, intellectual, and spiritual union; of "naked and unashamed" intimacy (Genesis 2:25). In Christ, couples may lay hold of His redemption of the marriage institution for their own marriages and experience the restoration of all that husbands and wives have lost because of sin. In the book of Ruth, Naomi introduces the notion of marriage as "rest" (Ruth 3:1, KJV). The Sabbath is a time of rest; marriage is a place of rest.

As is true of the Sabbath, we can experience marriage as God originally intended only when we enter into covenant relationship with Him as His children, receiving with reverence and joy this precious gift from the Creator Himself. In God's design, intimacy with one's marriage partner depends on intimacy with God. Temple Gairdner, an early Christian missionary to Cairo and a man of deep spiritual understanding, recorded this prayer in his diary as he prepared for his wedding: "That I may come near to her, draw me nearer to Thee than to her; that I may know her, make me to know Thee more than her; that I may love her with the perfect love of a perfectly whole heart, cause me to love Thee more than her and most of all. That nothing may be between me and her, be Thou between us, every moment. That we may be constantly together, draw us into separate loneliness with Thyself. And when we meet breast to breast, O God, let it be upon Thine own."[2]

Though human beings are drawn to the idea of oneness in marriage, because of sin we cannot in and of ourselves enter into this "naked and unashamed" one-fleshness. The fullness of couple life that was God's creation intent is born of the whole-hearted, self-giving investment of both partners in the relationship. But from Genesis 3 forward, selfishness on the parts of both husbands and wives has profoundly disrupted marriage relationships. In many marriages, self-interest and a struggle for power and control have well-nigh eclipsed the equality, mutuality, love, companionship, caring, and support that characterized the marriage relationship in Eden.

Women have borne a disproportionate share of the effects of sin on the marital relationship. Throughout history, in many societies, wives have been viewed as the property of their husbands. The lot of many women, in the home as well as in society, has been very difficult. Ellen White made the following comment on the hard consequences of the Fall: "After Eve's sin, as she was first in the transgression, the Lord told her that Adam should rule over her. She was to be in subjection to her husband, and this was a part of the curse."[3] In many places, gender inequalities and the maltreatment of women have become normative in the family and in the society, as though there is something inferior about the female sex. It's important to note Ellen White's clarification that the subjection was not because she was female, but because "she was first in the transgression."

It is also important to note that the subjection was not part of the original creation design but was a result of sin. One way to understand the pronouncement of God, "He [your husband] will rule over you" (Genesis 3:16), is to picture God, the Great Physician, putting a cast on the fractured marriage relationship in order to stabilize it. But God didn't intend this cast to be worn forever. It is necessary only until He can deal with the sin that puts the institution of marriage at risk—until He can heal the fractured relationship between husband and wife and make marriage as good as new.

Jesus is the "Sun of righteousness . . . with healing in his wings" (Malachi 4:2, KJV). He, not a change in God's original plan for marriage, is God's answer to transgression. In Him, the curse has come to an end. God intends for Christian marriage partners to enjoy marriage restored now, even as we await His return—just as we may experience healing and growth in every other aspect of our lives through the power of His Spirit (Matthew 12:28; 2 Corinthians 5:17; Galatians 1:4; Ephesians 3:17–19; Hebrews 6:5).

Marriage restored

"Marriage has been perverted by sin; but it is the purpose of the gospel to restore its purity and beauty."[4] This is good news! The curse has trampled upon marriage, but it doesn't reign forever. The curse is not the gospel! Throughout Scripture it is evident that God has not given up on marriage. Shafts of redemptive light pierce the canopy of darkness that shrouds the marriage institution even in the most troubled times. In the midst of the heartbreak of the Fall's impact on marriage, God provides the assurance of Christ's victory over Satan (Genesis 3:16).

Throughout the Old Testament, the "prophets exalted marriage, using it to describe God's love, and they decried the abuses that befell the God-ordained relationship. All parts of the Hebrew Scriptures celebrated romance and friendship as well as covenant faithfulness between husband and wife—in the Law, the Prophets, and the Writings."[5]

But with the advent of Jesus, the brightness of morning shines. He reaffirmed His creation intent for husband and wives: " 'Haven't you read,' " He asked the Pharisees, " 'that at the beginning the Creator "made them male and female," and said, "For this reason a man will leave his father and mother and be united to his wife, and the two will become one flesh"?' " (Matthew 19:4, 5). The New Testament views marriage as it is redeemed in Christ, proclaiming, "Marriage should be honored by all" (Hebrews 13:4).

In bridging the gulf between God and humanity, Christ also bridges the chasm sin created between human beings (2 Corinthians 5:18, 19). Even as He removes the barriers between heaven and earth, He removes the barriers between us. Paul declared that in Him, we transcend gender conflicts at home, at church, and in society (Galatians 3:28). Paul exalted the cross of Christ as the only source of reconciliation. In doing so, he used language that could as well apply to the separation between male and female as to the gulf between Jew and Gentile (Ephesians 2:14–18). Jesus died "to create out of the two a single new humanity in himself, thereby making peace" (Ephesians 2:15, NEB).

This is good news for marriage. It confronts the curse on marriage found in Genesis 3. In this "single new humanity," married couples, who are called to be "one flesh," may know the intimate oneness God originally intended. With the cross of Christ drawing them together, with Christ Himself linking them, they may experience a marriage as sweet as the one formed in Eden. The gospel calls us to grow up into Christ in all things (Ephesians 4:15). In Christ, couples can experience marriage as God meant it to be.

Created to be "us"

Christian marriage researcher Scott Stanley, in his profound book *The Heart of Commitment,* describes oneness in marriage. "The two," he says, "form a new, highly prized identity of 'us' that is to be nurtured and protected."[6] He continues, "People who are the most comfortable thinking in terms of 'we' tend to be the most dedicated and happy in their marriages."[7] "Marriage is about commingled lives. Marriage is about sharing and learning to share more."[8]

Stanley tells the story of Randy and June, who marry in their early thirties. Hardworking and successful career professionals, they have little time for church or for God, though they consider themselves Christians. Married life is good at first. They enjoy exercising, hiking, talking, and listening to music together. However, both have their own worlds, which they carefully guard. Five years into marriage, two crises develop. First, June's company decides to move across the country, and she will have to move with it if she wants to keep her position on the corporate ladder. Randy doesn't even want to discuss it; he's unwilling to consider any interruption to his own career.

As they fight with the question of whose career will take precedence and whether their commitment to one another can triumph over their personal investment in their individual careers, a second crisis hits. June learns that she is pregnant. It is altogether unplanned. Unsure of Randy's response, June at first hesitates to tell him. When she finally does, her worst fears are realized. He is angry and goes immediately into solution mode, wanting to explore "options" rather than share together from their innermost thoughts and feelings.

Convicted that abortion is not an option for her, June is deeply hurt. However, the immense pain that Randy sees in her face triggers something in him. That day he begins for the first time to think of letting go of his self-interest in consideration of the interests and well-being of his wife. He prays at work throughout the day, and so, it turns out, does she. By the time he reaches home that evening, Randy has done a turnabout. He confesses how self-centered his view of marriage has been, and then he says, "I don't think being married is all about me or you; it needs to be about us. I don't know how to do 'us,' but I'm willing to start learning. . . . I think I wanted this marriage only as long as it was good for both of us. I don't believe that's commitment. I want commitment. I want you to know I'll be by your side no matter what *we* decide to do. Will you *be married with me?* I mean, you and me together?"[9]

June responds with tears and hugs. The couple takes what could have been the end of their marriage and makes of it a new beginning.

The book of Ecclesiastes contains some wonderful lines about the beauty of partnerships: "Two are better than one; they receive a good reward for their toil, because, if one falls, the other can help his companion up again; but alas for the man who falls alone with no partner to help him up" (Ecclesiastes 4:9, 10, NEB).

Some of us, because of choice or circumstance, live life as single adults. But for all, God understands the human need for companionship and provides friends and the fellowship of the family of God. People need people for support and encouragement. Couples need other couples. So God planted us all in families and in the community of the church, where we can laugh and cry together and support, encourage, and nurture one another as the kingdom of God has come to us in Christ.

Remember Ben and Katie from our in-flight movie? After collecting the children and loading their camp gear into the car, Ben casts a knowing glance at Katie and says with resolution in his voice, "Let's go home." However, Katie doesn't follow Ben to the car. In a deeply moving soliloquy, she brings *The Story of Us* to a climax. But what she says is more about new beginnings than endings. "I don't think we should go home," she says, suggesting they go instead to the family's favorite restaurant. Ben is puzzled. This was not the plan. Is she just putting off telling the kids about the divorce?

No, she explains, she wants to go to the restaurant because they "are an 'us.' " They have history. They know one another's idiosyncrasies, can read one another's moods, and there's comfort in their well-worn routines. "That's a dance you perfect over time," she goes on. "And it's hard, much harder than I thought it would be, but there's more good than bad, and you don't just give up!" There are too many shared memories that would all be lost with a stranger for a husband. There's too much invested in these wonderful kids they have made together.

She's crying now as she admits aloud that she realizes nobody's perfect. All married couples have to find a way to deal with differentness. She acknowledges her part in the breakdown of the relationship and promises to try to do better. She wants to go to the restaurant, she says with conviction, "because I love you."

In the end, the experience of being an "us" carries the day. It helps both Katie and Ben to face themselves honestly and to recognize how their differing temperaments, personalities, and ways of doing things made of their marriage something wonderful, something neither of them could have known alone.

Christian couples know it is the presence of a divine Third Person entwined with their coupleness that enables this experience of "us" to be fully realized and to have staying power. As the wise man concludes: "If two lie side by side, they keep each other warm; but how can one keep warm by himself? If a man is alone, an assailant may overpower him, but two can resist; and a cord of three strands is not quickly snapped" (Ecclesiastes 4:9–12, NEB).

It was God's intent for the institution of marriage to bind together a man, a woman, and their Creator in a covenant never to be broken. As we surrender to Christ's love and the changing power of His grace in ourselves and in our relationships, it can be so again.

---

1. Ellen G. White, *Thoughts From the Mount of Blessing* (Nampa, Idaho: Pacific Press®, 1956), 63.

2. Quoted in David Mace and Vera Mace, *In the Presence of God: Readings for Christian Marriage* (Philadelphia, Penn.: The Westminster Press, 1985), 63.

3. Ellen G. White, *Testimonies for the Church* (Nampa, Idaho: Pacific Press®, 1948), 3:484.

4. White, *Thoughts From the Mount of Blessing,* 64.

5. Karen and Ron Flowers, *Love Aflame* (Hagerstown, Md.: Review and Herald, 1992), 81.

6. Scott Stanley, *The Heart of Commitment* (Nashville, Tenn.: Thomas Nelson Publishers, 1998), 8.

7. Stanley and Markman, "Assessing Commitment in Personal Relationships" as quoted in Stanley, *The Heart of Commitment,* 162.

8. Stanley, *The Heart of Commitment,* 165.

9. Ibid., 169.

Parenting Shepherd-Style

A brightly colored poster in a store window caught our attention. It announced an upcoming choral arts society performance of Handel's oratorio *Messiah.* We paused to get the details, savoring the memory of the first time we heard the full-length version of this musical masterpiece—redemption's story set in song.

"Comfort ye, comfort ye my people" (Isaiah 40:1, KJV) are the reassuring words of God with which both Isaiah and Handel open majestic pieces. Isaiah is known as "the gospel prophet," and the gospel *is* comfort for all—for the fearful and oppressed, the guilty who worry they may have sinned away their day of grace, the weak and weary who stagger under the weight of heavy burdens. Isaiah was speaking to Hebrews who would soon bear the crushing blow of foreign conquest and captivity. Handel understood, however, that Isaiah also spoke prophetically to people of every time and place.

Distressed families today may take comfort in these words, for Isaiah's prophecy points to Jesus, the Savior of the world. In Him there is solace for Andrew and Bethany, who grieve the loss of their college-age daughter in a tragic car accident. There is balm for Jose and Silvia, whose infant son was born with spina bifida. There is consolation for Tommy, Jason, and their dad, whose mother and wife, Julie, abruptly abandoned them, simply announcing she didn't want to be a wife and mother anymore.

The words "comfort my people" are there for those terrorized by war, stricken by disaster, and traumatized by abuse and internal strife that is shredding the very fabric of family itself. Take heart, said Isaiah. Help is on the way! The anticipated One has come (Isaiah 40:10).

As if to quell all doubt as to His ability to rescue, the prophet adds that He has come "with power, and his arm rules for him." Many of the subsequent verses describe the awe-inspiring strength and majesty of this Sovereign Lord. "He sits enthroned above the circle of the earth. . . . The LORD is the everlasting God" (Isaiah 40:22, 28). His cupped hands hold the oceans. His spread fingers span the heavens. He can carry earth's dust in a basket; He can weigh its mountains (Isaiah 40:12). He is the incomparable God. In Him the weak are made strong.

Into the midst of this description of divine might the prophet tucks an incredible concept that challenges typical notions of power and profoundly shapes our understanding of the Messiah and His ministry. Handel captured it in the air of Part the First, No. 20: "He shall feed his flock like a shepherd." This Deliverer, this Sovereign Lord, does not resemble any other magistrate the world has known. Rather, He will be shepherdlike. Said Isaiah, "He tends his flock like a shepherd: He gathers the lambs in his arms and carries them close to his heart; he gently leads those that have young" (Isaiah 40:11).

Jesus Himself embraced the shepherd identity. "I am the good shepherd," He explained (John 10:11, 14). Further expanding the metaphor, He fused the shepherd imagery with another prophetic view of the Messiah—that of suffering servant, One who in death bears the iniquities of all (see Isaiah 42; 49; 53). Jesus said, "The good shepherd lays down his life for the sheep" (John 10:11).

The religious leaders and people of Jesus' day found this idea of a shepherd-style savior—not to mention a dying one—hard to grasp. Their Messianic expectations ran toward freedom from Roman occupation and recovery of the glory days of King David. We still cannot get our minds around this mystery of the incarnation of God—this unique joining of sovereignty and service in Christ described first by Isaiah. Even we who have seen and believed must accept it by faith. In Jesus was all the fullness of the Deity in bodily form (Colossians 2:9), yet He "made himself nothing, taking the very nature of a servant" (Philippians 2:7). It's incomprehensible, but true.

As the Good Shepherd, Jesus has intimate knowledge of His people's nature and habits. He gently guides them in safe paths, compassionately cares for their needs, and finds them when they stray. The prophetic description of the shepherd's care for the lambs and their mothers is particularly meaningful for families, for it aptly describes Jesus' personal response to children and parents of all time: "He gathers the lambs in his arms and carries them close to his heart; he gently leads those that have young" (Isaiah 40:11).

Close are the lambs to His heart

Real-life lambs are winsome. They draw out our caring instincts. Far more vulnerable to predators and disease than are the adults of the flock, they provide God with an apt metaphor for children of the human species.

Jesus loves children. Whenever they turned up, no matter how important His agenda, He stopped and gave them His attention. In a statement with staggering implications, He identified Himself with children: "Whoever welcomes one of these little children in my name welcomes me; and whoever welcomes me does not welcome me but the one who sent me" (Mark 9:37). At that moment, He forever established an elevated status for children, letting all who have contact with them know that what they do to the least of these, they do to Him.

Perhaps the most outstanding example in our time of one who lived life by this reality was Agnes Bojaxhiu, better known to the world as Mother Teresa. She worked with the poor of Calcutta, a large measure of whom were children. In each one she saw the face of Jesus Christ. As she put it, she was all the while "loving Him in His miserable disguise." At the 331st commencement of Harvard University, she brought her understanding to the family doorstep when she challenged her audience: "We must have the courage to recognize that the poor you may have *right in your own family*. Find them, love them, put your love for them in a loving action. For in loving them, *you are loving God himself*."[1]

Like so many of us, Jesus' disciples were slow to grasp His vision. As parents brought their little ones to Him, the disciples blocked their access. They thought that they were doing right by guarding the Lord from distraction. Scripture describes Jesus' quick and indignant corrective reaction: " 'Let the little children come to me, and do not hinder them, for the kingdom of God belongs to such as these' " (Mark 10:14).

The people were bringing their children to Jesus because they wanted Him to touch them (Mark 10:13). In Bible times, touching the head of a child with the hand was a special parental gesture of blessing. Jacob, for example, thus blessed his grandsons Ephraim and Manasseh (Genesis 48:13–18). Many Jewish parents today maintain the tradition of blessing their children, especially on the Sabbath, by resting a hand on their heads and reciting words of affirmation and goodwill. Such frequent blessing and affirmation is no doubt a major factor in the strong family ties characterizing Jewish families.

The parents and extended family who accompanied the children into Jesus' presence heard His words, but they also *saw* what He did. Jesus touched children, but He did more than merely touch their heads. In a tender word picture of the Divine Shepherd, Mark says specifically that He took them "in his arms" (Mark 9:36; 10:16). The nonverbal gesture of picking up children—encircling them in your arms, elevating them to your height, bringing their face close to your face, their eyes reflected in your own—communicates respect, affection, and protection. Such close body contact with Jesus spoke volumes to the kids and their parents about His love and the value He placed on each one.

In the children's innocence and trusting nature, Jesus saw the faith He yearned to inspire in all His followers. He determined to protect that purity and willing dependence. His words in defense of vulnerable children are among the strongest in Scripture: " 'If anyone causes one of these little ones who believe in me to sin, it would be better for him to have a large millstone hung around his neck and to be drowned in the depths of the sea' " (Matthew 18:6).

We once heard a heart-wrenching report of a misguided father who beckoned his child to jump from a lofty place into his waiting arms. Hesitant at first because of the height, the trusting child eventually leaped toward him. As he did so, the father withdrew his arms and stepped back, allowing the child to fall to the ground. Fortunately, the child was not seriously injured, but he was terrified and horribly confused. "That will teach you an important lesson," was the father's only comment. "Never trust anybody."

Any hurtful attitudes or actions can make it very difficult for children to place their trust in God. All abusive treatment—physical, emotional, or sexual, especially at the hands of a parent—is tantamount to unspeakable betrayal. Its effects penetrate to the innermost core of the child's being and often shape behavior for a lifetime. Because parents represent God to their children, a crisis of faith often ensues that frequently results in difficulty trusting friends or a marriage partner. Only an experience of God's grace in a healing, life-affirming environment—with the guidance of licensed counselors wherever possible—can enable children and adults with such scars to find healing.

Reflection on Jesus' attitude and teachings regarding children has led many Christians to a keen awareness of the potential for physical and psychological abuse in some approaches to child discipline. Striking a child's body or depriving a child physically or emotionally may result in compliance, but it often generates negative feelings and adverse reactions. Christ's warning and other biblical instruction not to exasperate children (Ephesians 6:4) stand as strong counsel to parents, for "children are the heritage of the Lord, and we are answerable to Him for our management of His property."[2]

Leading gently those with young

Few joys compare with that of joining the Creator in the formation of a new person and experiencing the wonder of life alongside a growing child. Our two sons are true "love children." We wanted them. Our photograph albums testify to the delight we take in them and to the memories we've made as a family. The setting for some of the best of those memories was the backyard treehouse we built together. You entered it by climbing up the tree and pushing yourself through a trapdoor in the floor. The treehouse had shuttered windows and was carpeted with leftovers from the recarpeting of our family room. It was the envy of neighborhood kids, and some of the dads made it clear that Ron hadn't made life easier for them! It was just big enough for the four of us. We enjoyed the squeezing, enhanced by snacks catered by Mom. That tiny dwelling was the site of some of our most memorable times together.

Like all parents, though, we too have felt the weightiness of parenting. Ron recalls the first time he saw our firstborn, Jeff, in the hospital nursery. He remembers a load settling on his shoulders as the thought sank in, *You're responsible for this little life.* We've known the mixed feelings of most parents as our sons have ventured away from home and moved into new seasons of their lives. We've stood beside friends who've suffered through grave illness and life-changing tragedy with their children. We've shed tears over the graves of children lost in death long before they had enjoyed the expected measure of life. We've counseled parents who have had to cope with runaways, with calls to juvenile court, and with a child's persistence in risky behaviors involving sex and drugs. We know the bewilderment that sweeps over all parents at one point or another about what they have done wrong and what they should do next.

Jesus' words and actions refreshed the spirits of all those who pressed their little ones close to Him.[3] He affirmed mothers and fathers alike, encouraging them in their parenting. He wants to lift the weariness and worry that burden us as well. However difficult a child might be right now, however taxing the load of parenting, we can know for certain that Jesus loves that child, that He loves us, and that He wants to love the child through us.

Ours is the priceless opportunity to bring our children into His presence as much as it is in our power to do so—to pray for them and with them and to winsomely invite them to meet this One whom we know as Savior and Lord. When we're at our extremity, we can press them into His arms. He will reach out to them with an unconditional acceptance and grace that transcends our own. He longs to lavish His blessing and every good gift upon them in like measure to everything we long to bestow. His heart is compassionately in tune with our own.

Jesus ever sought to strengthen the bonds of attachment between parents and their children and to restore normalcy to the family experiencing tragedy and disruption. With compassion for the widow of Nain, He ended the mournful march of the funeral procession to raise her son to life (Luke 7:11–15). When a nobleman from Capernaum interceded with Jesus on behalf of his dying son, Jesus performed a miracle that altered life in their household forever (John 4:46–53).

Especially in need of the divine Shepherd's care are parents who have invested heavily in their children, only to have them reject the values they hold dear. Our heavenly Parent knows all about this experience. As He looked across the valley at the city that personified children dear to His heart, He wept. He experienced all the emotions parents feel when children ignore counsel, behave in disappointing ways, and turn their backs on home. "The hardest part of love is letting go" wrote Stephen Schwartz in the musical *Children of Eden*.[4] But God places such a high value on human freedom that even when children's choices set them on a path away from Him, He respects their decision. Meanwhile, He sustains parents whose tears and heartache intermingle with His own as they reluctantly respect their children's decisions too. He will guide those parents in knowing whether or how to seek after a wayward son or daughter—when to go like the shepherd in search of a lost sheep, and when to wait patiently at the gate with the father of the prodigal.

How would the Good Shepherd raise a child?

Jesus Himself was not a parent—that is to say, He did not father children. We find preposterous the best-selling novel, purportedly rooted in historical fact, that smears the character of Christ by contending that He sired a child by Mary Magdalene and that the Christian church has engaged in a cover-up ever since. Yet Christ did model a parental role. Says Teresa Whitehurst, "As we observe how Jesus mentored his disciples, we have a model for parenting our children that is radically different from contemporary models."[5]

We might, for example, look to His relationship to the high-spirited, hot-tempered disciple John for answers. Knowing John's inner hunger for love, Jesus—as John later marveled—*kept on* loving him with unconditional love (*agapē*) in spite of his feisty character

45

(John 13:23; 19:26; 21:7, 20). Jesus not only loved John, Scripture says He *liked* him—He felt toward him a fondness (from *philos,* the Greek word for the love of friends; see John 20:2). He pulled John in close to Himself, into an inner circle of disciples with Peter and James. He spent time with them, talked at length with them. In His most vulnerable moment in Gethsemane, Jesus opened Himself to them, depended on their support and encouragement.

Jesus was both *kind* and *firm* with John.* When the young man strayed, Jesus corrected him with love (Matthew 20:22–24; Luke 9:52–56). Though He openly confronted the misbehavior, He didn't shame John. Rather, He clarified the principles of life in His kingdom family. When Jesus hung on the cross, He entrusted to John responsibility for the care of His own mother. The legacy of His relationship with John is woven into the fabric of history—in the leadership John gave to the church and in his writings, which, not surprisingly, speak more of love than do those of any other Gospel writer.

Some time ago we purchased a video titled *Matthew,* a filmed version of the Gospel of Matthew that uses only the biblical text as its script. We are particularly moved by the footage of the leper whose story is told in Matthew 8:1–4. Walking along a dirt road toward Capernaum, Jesus hears a muffled cry, "Lord, if You are willing, You can make me clean." The sound emanates from a wretched shell of a man, a social outcast whose disease in biblical times epitomized sin itself. Everyone recoils from him, some shout at him, but Jesus stops everything to connect with him. At His approach, the leper turns his face away and falls to his knees. Jesus lowers Himself down before him, bringing His face close enough to feel the leper's breath. Tenderly the Master lifts the diseased chin in His hand so that His eyes can meet those of the leper. Carefully He unwraps the grimy rag-mask required by Jewish law

---

*The concepts of *kindness* and *firmness,* which frequently appear in tandem in Ellen G. White's writings on parenting, closely parallel the characteristics of authoritative parenting, which is often described in contemporary parenting literature as the most effective style: "In order to maintain . . . authority, it is not necessary to resort to harsh measures; a *firm,* steady hand and a *kindness* which convinces the child of your love will accomplish the purpose." (Ellen G. White, *Child Guidance* [Hagerstown, Md.: Review and Herald, 1954], 283, emphasis supplied.)

and tosses it aside. Then, flashing a warm smile, Jesus says kindly, "I am willing; be clean."

As damaged nerve-endings reconnect and surge with energy, the invigorated leper begins to dance and leap about with childish exuberance. He runs to Jesus, throwing his arms about His neck. His momentum knocks them both over, and they roll together by the roadside, both of them delirious with joy.

In his book *In the Footsteps of Jesus,* Bruce Marchiano wrote about the transforming experience of acting the part of Christ. As he prepared for each scene, he prayed that he might know the mind and heart of Jesus and interact with the various people as Jesus would have. When he thought about the leper, it dawned on him that this was a living, breathing, human being. He was "a man with a name and history; hopes, dreams, and desires; with a mother, father, maybe even a wife and kids."[6] Then a breathtaking awareness engulfed the actor and compelled him to enact the scene as he did: Jesus "created that leper. He knew that leper's name. . . . That leper 2000 years ago was His very own child."[7]

Shepherdlike care is the hallmark of Jesus' attitude and actions for all of sinful, fallen humanity. Each one is His very own child. Jesus summons us also to shepherd our flocks. Not every child responded to His love, as Judas illustrates. Ours may not either. But Jesus keeps on loving, and so must we.

Perhaps the best news for parents is that this wonderful Good Shepherd is yet accessible. He is there for all parents who need help to know how to guide their youth, or who perhaps need reparenting themselves in the presence of the kind of healing, restoring love only Jesus can provide. He is there for youth, challenged by difficult intrapersonal and interpersonal issues, some of whom may never have a parent or mentor to walk beside them on their journey into adulthood. He is ever present and can always be found, offering comfort and encouragement in His Word, in a quiet moment of prayer and reflection, in the presence of His Spirit.

He is there for you.

---

1. Teresa Whitehurst, *Jesus on Parenting* (Grand Rapids, Mich.: Baker Books, 2003), 10.

2. Ellen G. White, *The Adventist Home* (Hagerstown, Md.: Review and Herald, 1952), 159.

3. Ibid., 273, 274.

4. Stephen Schwartz, "The Hardest Part of Love Is Letting Go," *Children of Eden.*

5. Whitehurst, 33.

6. Bruce Marchiano, *In the Footsteps of Jesus* (Eugene, Ore.: Harvest House Publishers, 1997), 94.

7. Ibid., 95.

Knowing Heavenly Father

"I've never known Him as a God of love," the elderly man lamented to his pastor. In his retirement, this man had taken his church under his wing and become a kind of father to it. He was its only local elder. Upon him rested the responsibility for preaching and leading the worship service whenever the pastor was busy with other congregations in his large district.

But the elder was temperamental—at times winsome, but often distant and hard, and complaints swirled among the members. As Sabbath School teacher, the old man scolded them for their deficiencies in Bible knowledge, their tardiness, and the lack of enthusiasm in their singing. The dwindling group, hard-pressed to find willing help, had reluctantly made him the treasurer too. With the additional power this afforded him, he would rail at the members about their lack of faithfulness in returning their tithes and giving offerings. And when their faces grew long, he frowned again, admonishing them for not being happy, smiling Christians. Members sighed and complained among themselves, "He *never* preaches about the love of God." If visitors came, it was usually only once, and in time, even the "regulars" became noticeably absent.

"Please, pastor," pleaded an elderly widow one day, "don't let this man preach to us anymore. He has the whole church in the palm of his hand, and he's squeezing it until all its juices are running down between his fingers!" That day the pastor decided he must visit the old elder. After the usual pleasantries, the pastor confronted him with the members' concerns. "They just want to hear more about God's love," the pastor explained. "People really do need to hear about God's love." At first the elder went silent. Then, unexpectedly, deep, uncontrollable sobs welled up from the core of his being.

After a few minutes he pulled himself together and, gazing out the window, launched into a story about a little boy and his dad. The lad so much wanted love and affection from his father, but his father always pushed him away. There were no words of kindness, no expressions of appreciation or affirmation—even when his report card was really good or when he diligently finished his chores. All the little boy had hoped for was an affectionate hug, a pat on the head, a touch of love, but it was never to be. "There wasn't time for such silly games." Worse, he never knew when he might be slapped for no reason he could account for, or even kicked and told to get away.

It took the pastor a few minutes to make sense of it all, but everything became clear as it broke over him that this was not just a story. The hard old elder was himself the little boy! He never said so, but the vivid detail, his tears, the pain in his voice gave everything away. The story was as fresh as if it had taken place yesterday.

The pastor listened as the aged lay leader rambled on for some time about this sad family, still telling his tale in third-person pronouns. Then, abruptly, he made his confession in the first person: "They say God is a God of love. I've never known Him as a God of love."

As the old saying goes, "What goes around comes around." Life in the family in which the elder grew up had profoundly shaped his view of the world and of the spiritual realm where God dwells. Unfortunately, this shadow over the face of God was much more than just a personal tragedy. Its results rippled in ever-widening circles, affecting the well-being of all who came in contact with this man—family, friends, congregation, and even community.

Seeing through a child's eyes

It's so important to see things through children's eyes. Child-development specialists can help us understand how children reach conclusions about their world, especially the spiritual world. Their insights have profound implications for anyone close to children.

Armand Nicholi writes, "Early family experience determines our adult character structure, the inner picture we harbor of ourselves, how we see others and feel about them, our concept of right and wrong, our capacity to establish the close, warm, sustained relationships necessary to have a family of our own, our attitude toward authority and toward the Ultimate Authority in our lives, and the way we attempt to make sense out of our existence. No human interaction has a greater impact on our lives than our family experience."[1]

Children first imagine God as being like their parents, especially their father. They view everyone bigger and older and in authority through the lens of the big people they know. The big people most central in their lives are their parents or those who stand in as parents. *So this God-person,* the children reason, *must be like my mommy and daddy. And,* as childish logic goes, *since people call this God-person "Father," He must be especially like my father.*

Richard Strauss, in his excellent book *How to Raise Confident Children,* adds these insights: "If [a person's] parents were happy, loving, accepting, and forgiving, he finds it easier to experience a positive and satisfying relationship with God. But if his parents were cold and indifferent, he may feel that God is far away and disinterested in him personally. If his parents were angry, hostile, and rejecting, he often feels that God can never accept him. If his parents were hard to please, he usually has the nagging notion that God is not very happy with him either."[2]

When the elder was a small boy, life in the family had been hard. Parental love—children's most fundamental emotional need—had been scarce at best, often confusing, and at worst, withheld all together. Perhaps his parents would have argued that they *did* love him—he had a roof over his head and food on his plate, didn't he? Perhaps overwork strained the family's resources of time and emotional energy. Perhaps the parents had more children with more emotional needs than they could meet. Maybe they held the misguided belief that the best way to prepare kids for the real world is to apply harsh, punitive discipline. Or they may have only been playing out the parenting model they experienced as children. The point is that this little boy didn't *feel* loved, and, as time passed, that feeling embedded itself deep within him and profoundly affected all his relationships—with God and with other human beings.

There are many who could slip easily into the old elder's childhood shoes. Perhaps problems at home, even at church, have shaded or blocked your view of God and insulated you from the warmth of His love. Images of home and family may make it difficult, even impossible, for you to call God "Father," even when you pray. Maybe you continue to go to church and try to make the whole religion thing work despite this handicap. Perhaps you, like many others, "have taken a break from church." Maybe experiences in your family of origin and perhaps the religious milieu with which you are most familiar simply make it too painful to participate.

I [Ron] baptized my father a few years before he died in his eighties. From his early adulthood, he had nothing to do with religion. All those years must have been difficult for him. His parents, my grandparents, had a very large family. Life during the Great Depression was hard. From stories I've heard, I know emotional warmth was at a premium. Ardent new Adventists, my father's parents held leadership positions in the church that absorbed what little free time they had. Boundaries were completely blurred: parentschurch-religionGod were one and the same to Dad. Deeply hurt by family experiences, he sought to escape the pain by severing ties with his parents and most of his siblings. In the process, he also cut himself off from religion and the church.

Late in life, his heart softened. A caring pastor who knew God as a God of love was in the right place in God's time. He discerned the deep needs of my father's heart—for love, warmth, acceptance, forgiveness, and release from past hurts and for relationships with people who had tasted God's goodness. He invited my dad, a skilled carpenter and builder, to superintend the construction of the new church building. Dad liked this man and readily took on the job. At some point the realization settled upon him that he, like Solomon, was building a house for God. When it was finished, he worshipped Him there. It wasn't long before I got the call. He wanted me to baptize him!

The story of the elder ends similarly. Sharing his story with the pastor proved to be a kind of turning point for him, starting him off on a journey toward personal healing and new beginnings with God and the congregation. It was a miracle of grace.

God in the neighborhood

Over time, a grand thought has taken shape for us, sifted from the writings of several authors. It began to form when we read *The Embrace of God,* in which Adventist clinical psychologist Lloyd Erickson ministers lovingly to those for whom the word *father* calls up difficult memories.[3] He gently lures the reader away from the stagnant reservoir of negative images that persist in their minds, introducing them to a warm, loving Person who wants more than anything else to enjoy our friendship. Erickson calls God "Heavenly Father" rather than "*the* heavenly Father." This simple shift in language brought new insights to us. Heavenly Father wants to fold us into a loving embrace as no one has before.

An article by Lynda Barry in *Newsweek* also captured our attention. She told of growing up in a troubled family with troubled families for neighbors. For the most part, healthy family relationships seemed like a fairy tale. Then a family in which things were different moved in. Their home drew the kids in the neighborhood like a magnet. Once Lynda showed up on their doorstep and announced that she had come for breakfast. These neighbors invited her in. During the meal, she saw the wife kiss her husband as she served up his toast and eggs, and she saw the father pull his son onto his lap and hold him close, as if this were the most natural thing in the world. She had never seen love openly expressed like this before. She wrote, "That was all I needed to see. I only needed to see it once to be able to believe for the rest of my life that happiness between two people can exist."[4]

These images mingle in our minds with the words of the brash young disciple John, whose heart was warmed by Jesus' love. Listen to his invitation:

> From the very first day, we were there, taking it all in—we heard it with our own ears, saw it with our own eyes, verified it with our own hands. The Word of Life appeared right before our eyes; we saw it happen! And now we're telling you in most sober prose that what we witnessed was, incredibly, this: The infinite Life of God himself took shape before us.
>
> We saw it, we heard it, and now we're telling you so you can experience it along with us, this experience of communion

with the Father and his Son, Jesus Christ. Our motive for writing is simply this: We want you to enjoy this, too. Your joy will double our joy! (1 John 1:1–4, TM)

If we distill the Christian message to its essence, it is the story of a warm, affectionate Father who has moved into our neighborhood. He throws the door to His place wide open, inviting in all passersby. There is love where He is! If you've not experienced love before, you'll find it here. You'll only need to encounter love once for your life to be changed forever. Heavenly Father will reparent everyone whose life so far has been difficult and forgettable. Having experienced love firsthand, you'll have a full measure to offer your children. In fact, God invites your children too. There are no age limits, no socioeconomic requirements, no racial barriers. He extends His invitation to all! Come, join the others inside who are reveling in what they've found.

We meet Heavenly Father through knowing Jesus. Wrote John, "The Word became flesh and blood, and moved into the neighborhood. We saw the glory with our own eyes, the one-of-a-kind glory, like Father, like Son, generous inside and out, true from start to finish" (John 1:14, TM; cp. John 14:9). With imagery unused on earth before, Jesus identified God as "Father." Jesus wants to introduce you to God, His Father—who is also your Father and ours (John 20:17).

Don't wait. Take your Bible. Use a contemporary-language version for a change. Walk along with Jesus in the pages of the Gospels. Listen to Him. Let Him introduce you to Heavenly Father. In Jesus, God bends low to whisper gently in the ear of everyone whose family experience—at home, at church, or wherever—has been tough. "I love you," He says. He means it, too. *He loves you.* You can trust that.

Helping children and youth toward discipleship

We recently adopted another grandchild. In our unbiased opinion, she is the most beautiful two-year-old in the world. As we posted her Christmas present, we enclosed a note thanking her mom and dad for including us in the circle of family who will have the privilege of introducing little Selene to Jesus. It's the most important work ever bestowed on humankind. How can parents do it?

Love God, and share your passion. "Love the LORD your God with all your heart," Moses coached parents. "These commandments . . . are to be upon your hearts. Impress them on your children" (Deuteronomy 6:5–7). Children rarely heed the command "Don't do as I do—do as I say" for the simple reason that values are caught more than they are taught. As the truism goes, "an apple rarely falls far from the tree."

While we were conducting a seminar in Bali, a procession of fifty or more people caught our attention. In the front were men carrying banners, waving their hands, and chanting in unison to the beat of drums and tambourines. Women came next, dancing and chanting responsively. And bringing up the rear were the children—boys ahead, girls behind. Zooming in on this last part of the procession was like watching the front half in miniature. The boys mimicked everything their fathers did, and the girls mimicked their mothers.

We were told this was a Hindu-Bali religious rite of some kind. It was not hard at all to see why, at that time at least, not one person from among the Hindu-Bali people had converted to Adventism. From the children's youngest years, the unique form of Hinduism practiced there had been imprinted on them. It formed a values-hold very difficult to break. Christian values are ever so much more winsome, but our children will buy them most readily when the spiritual exhibits of our own lives are too alluring to resist.

Warm your family with a loving marriage. In the farmhouse in eastern Canada where Ron grew up, heat rose into the kitchen and the living room through a large walkover register in the floor. On cold winter mornings, the kids both wanted a turn standing on the steel grate, letting the warm air puff out their skirts or pant legs. David and Vera Mace, founders of the marriage-enrichment movement in America, use this very imagery for a loving marriage: "Mutual affection between husband and wife will be to the family what the heating system is to a house. It will maintain the relationship of all family members in a pleasant and comfortable atmosphere."[5]

Such love is one of God's primary means of "warming up" a family spiritually. Ellen White wrote, "If the husband and wife would only continue to cultivate these attentions which nourish love, they would . . . have a sanctifying influence upon their families."[6] Such "attentions" might be as simple as a kind word of appreciation, the cheerful sharing of household chores, a loving touch in the presence of the children, a warm smile exchanged silently across the dinner table, a birthday or anniversary card presented while the family is together, a gift or romantic getaway given with the children in on planning the surprise. Even children living with one parent following a divorce or separation monitor the relationship between their parents. Both parents represent a part of themselves. They need their father and mother to demonstrate respect for one another as persons.

Love them in. "No one will ever enter the kingdom of God except he is loved in," H. M. S. Richards, founder of *The Voice of Prophecy* radio program, used to say. Surveys of church dropouts indicate that many still affirm the beliefs of the church. They left because they didn't find fellowship there. Doctrines are important (Titus 2:1), but church is about connectedness, *koinōnia*—being folded into a loving community (Acts 2:42; 1 John 1:3–7).

Parental love is the template upon which a child's view of God's love is constructed. Psychologist Ross Campbell has helped many parents communicate their love to their children through focused attention, eye contact, appropriate touch, and listening to both their words and their feelings.[7]

Our good friend Harold explains how his teenage daughter Cheryl taught him about focused attention. She came into the room where he was reading a book and asked, "Can I talk to you, Dad?"

"Sure," Harold replied, keeping the book open on his lap.

"Dad," she commanded, "close your book."

Harold closed the book but used his finger to mark his place. Not to be denied his undivided attention, Cheryl insisted, "Dad, take your finger out of the book!"

Build a friendship with your child. Parents can't really be "best buddies" with their children, for there is an appropriate generation boundary between parents and children that it's crucial that parents keep in place. But parents can and should be friends with their children. The English word *like* gets at the idea of friendship. Children know when they are liked, and they're drawn to those who really like them. Kids need parents who are interested in what's going on in their lives, who know their friends by name, who are available when they need to talk, who share the important events in their lives, and who work and play alongside them.

Jesus cultivated friendship with His disciples. "I have called you friends," He said, "for everything that I learned from my Father I have made known to you" (John 15:15). The disciples could risk opening themselves to Jesus because they saw in Him a ready acceptance. They felt a complete assurance that He loved them, in both their strengths and weaknesses. Our friendship with our children helps them grasp how they can be friends with Jesus.

Be an askable parent. When God made a path through the Jordan, Joshua instructed twelve men to each pick up a stone from the riverbed and carry it to the other side. With those stones they built an altar so that "in the future, when your children ask you, 'What do these stones mean?' " parents could tell them about God's mighty act of making a path through the river (see Joshua 4). Joshua knew that children learn by asking questions.

Any question a child asks creates a prime teachable moment. Being an askable parent doesn't mean you will always have a ready answer. Rather, it means that your children know that you will take their questions seriously and respond in ways that do not belittle them for asking.

Children and teens are sometimes overlooked as fitting recipients of gospel-sharing efforts. We can't take it for granted that children and young people will automatically absorb all they need to know by living with Christian parents. These younger members of the Lord's family need a personal introduction to Jesus. It's our best hope that the next generation will know Heavenly Father and follow Him by faith.

---

1. Armand Nicholi II, "The Fractured Family: Following It into the Future," *Christianity Today,* May 25, 1979, 11.

2. Richard L. Strauss, *How to Raise Confident Children* (Grand Rapids, Mich.: Baker Book House, 1975), 23, 24.

3. See M. Lloyd Erickson, *The Embrace of God* (Minneapolis, Minn.: Bethany House Publishers, 1996).

4. Lynda Barry, "Guardian Neighbor," *Newsweek,* special issue, Summer 1991, 70–72.

5. David and Vera Mace, *In the Presence of God* (Philadelphia, Penn.: The Westminster Press, 1985), 109.

6. Ellen G. White, *Mind, Character and Personality* (Hagerstown, Md.: Review and Herald, 1977), 1:158.

7. See Ross Campbell, *How to Really Love Your Children* (New York: International Press, 1996).

Driving Lessons

One summer we decided to combine a working trip to England with a family vacation. As Americans are likely to do, we rented a car and set out to "conquer" the British Isles in two weeks. None of us had any experience driving on the left, so we nominated Ron to figure it out "on the go." It is not stretching the truth one bit to say that the rest of the family alternated between trepidation and earnest efforts at patience. Advice flowed freely, and our "nice batteries" struggled more than once to hold their charge.

The multilane highways were challenging enough to negotiate, but anxiety peaked on the two-lane country roads! While Ron concentrated on mentally measuring the distance between his door and on-coming traffic, his bent toward an unconscious drift to the left kept Jeff alert to the perils of the curb and ditch outside his window. "Dad, move over! You're going to hit the curb!" or "We're off the pavement over here!" were cries with which we became quite familiar.

Wisdom on the highway

Reading Proverbs is like having your own driving coach or finding a manual of useful travel tips for the highway of life. The Hebrew word for "way" appears more than sixty times in Proverbs. Generally, it denotes a way of life. As there's a right way to drive on the highway in every country, so there is a right way to travel the road of life—and there's a wrong way. The book of Proverbs sets these two ways of life in contrast to one another. One—"the ways of good men" (Proverbs 2:20)—is wise, upright, moral, and honorable. The other—"the way of the wicked" (Proverbs 4:19)—is its exact opposite: foolish, evil, corrupt, and unjust.

Not only does Proverbs provide wisdom for family living, it also models practical means of connecting with children and youth that best create the likelihood that they will make wise choices themselves when they're out of their parents' sight. It engages reason. It uses storytelling and asks thought-provoking questions. It makes the reader smile with witty comments that accurately depict the truth about living in close relationships even in this far-distant time and place.

Proverbs emphasizes our God-given power of choice. And just as the emergency lighting marks the aisle of an airplane, it illuminates the boundaries within which the godly person stays. It makes the reader clearly understand that consequences follow choices, and what those consequences—both good and bad—will be. It informs us that calamity is inevitable for those who stray off the good path. Go the wrong way, and you can expect to become a statistic, or at least risk serious injury to yourself and those who accompany you. Stay within the bounds—"keep 'er 'tween the poles," as Ron's father used to say—and you will reap handsome rewards both in the present and in the end.

Proverbs is written as a family document that passes down, as God intended, from parent to child, the success secrets of a godly life: "Listen, my son, to your father's instruction and do not forsake your mother's teaching" (Proverbs 1:8). My [Ron's] father taught me how to drive when I was five. Better, I should say, he taught me how to steer. During the potato harvest in the fields where he worked in northern Maine, he would take me on his lap and let me hold the steering wheel as his truck moved among the picking crew, loading up their barrels full of potatoes.

As I grew older, he'd sit beside me, letting me drive longer distances by myself, carefully choosing the open fields with no obstacles. The pull-type throttle compensated for my too-short legs that couldn't reach the gas pedal. I knew his foot was never far from the brake. Most of the farm boys I knew learned to drive this way. Long before we got our driver's licenses, we were regularly handling tractors and trucks on our farms, deftly working clutches, accelerators, gearshifts, and brakes.

Proverbs takes seriously the responsibility God gave parents to share their most cherished values with the next generation (Deuteronomy 6:4–9). Scripture recognizes the family as the primary place where values are caught. Just as a parent might write a letter to a son or daughter going off to college, setting up a house, or taking a job in a distant place, so the wise father of Proverbs addresses his offspring as he goes forth into the wider world. Behind the voice of this earthly father, we may also hear Heavenly Father calling all of us as His children to listen and learn.

Go to God heart-first

The foundation stone of all wisdom in Proverbs is laid early: "Trust in the LORD with all your heart, and lean not on your own understanding; in all your ways acknowledge Him, and He shall direct your paths" (Proverbs 3:5, 6, NKJV).

The sense of being invincible is a common human feeling that runs particularly strong in youth, when the I-can-do-it-myself determination of a two-year-old recycles at an all-time high. Youth perceive their own resources as sufficient. Fortunately, few have gone to the extreme of Oklahoma City bomber Timothy McVeigh, who left the words of William Henley's poem "Invictus" (Latin for "unconquerable") as his last message before his execution. But many men and women have lived at least a season of their lives in tune with the poem's last lines: "I am the master of my fate; I am the captain of my soul." Proverbs would dissuade us from this godless, self-centered attitude and urge us to put God at the center, to make Him captain of our souls.

An ancient rabbi described the words of Proverbs 3:5, 6 as "the text upon which 'all the essential principles of Judaism may be considered to hinge.' "[1] Christianity likewise. Christians see God as the Provider of all human needs (Matthew 6:8, 28–32; Philippians 4:19). They trust in the Son of God for salvation (Acts 16:31), and they seek His kingdom first of all (Matthew 6:25–34). Charles Wesley's gospel hymn "Jesus, Lover of My Soul" captures the essential God-trust that marks all of life for a Christian: "Other refuge have

I none, / Hangs my helpless soul on Thee. . . . / All my trust on Thee is stayed, / All my help from Thee I bring."[2]

Another cornerstone of wisdom in Proverbs sounds like a billboard for the national heart association. "Above all else, guard your heart, for it is the wellspring of life" (Proverbs 4:23). To the Hebrews, "heart" meant "mind," the intellectual and spiritual center of a person. Biblically, the condition of the heart defines individuals and determines the nature of their actions. Jesus taught, "Out of the overflow of his heart his mouth speaks" (Luke 6:45).

The natural human heart inclines away from God. The good news of the gospel is that Christ triumphed over Satan and sin (John 14:30; Romans 8:3). In Him, we too have victory. Paul wrote that as believers claim Christ's life and death for themselves and invite His Spirit to dwell with them, "you . . . are controlled not by the sinful nature but by the Spirit, if the Spirit of God lives in you" (Romans 8:9). God calls believers to live as though their sinful heart is dead, their corrupt nature crucified, though it will be finally eradicated only when our Lord returns (Romans 8:13; Galatians 2:20; Colossians 3:5; 1 Corinthians 15:53). Thus, the heart must be continually guarded and submitted to Christ (Galatians 5:17–25; cp. 1 Corinthians 9:27; 15:31). The temptation to choose another master is ever present, but looking to Jesus, we are safe. "Nothing can pluck us out of His hand."[3]

A lone shoe sticks in Ron's mind as a grim reminder of the importance of the counsel of Proverbs. He had an older cousin who in late adolescence lost interest in spiritual things. His heart inclined toward cars, fast cars. He had two new ones—a brand-new model one year that he promptly wrecked, and another the next. Ron's uncle purchased each in an effort to hold on to this son who was literally speeding out of control. Speed caught up with him one night on a sharp curve. The remains of the candy-apple red Chevrolet were towed to a local garage. The remains of the young man were prepared for burial in a small graveyard near his home. Reality hit hard when Ron peered inside what had been his cousin's car and saw the shoe, torn from his foot by the force of the impact. One shoe—all that was left of a son, a life, a heart bent on going its own way.

In Proverbs, everything depends upon the condition of the heart. The attractions of sin—whether sex, sloth, wealth, or power—abound. But the wise go to God heart-first, with hands unclasped to receive His very present help to make right choices—for the moment and for a lifetime.

Love choices

Heart advice is followed by a discussion in Proverbs 5 of one of life's most important choices—how to direct the capacity for love and lovemaking that the Creator has given us. In this passage the wise man once again contrasts right and wrong and the consequences that attend each. A man's lovemaking with a woman not his wife—the "wrong" woman—is juxtaposed with lovemaking with his wife—the "right" woman. The counsel applies to both married and unmarried. That is to say, married people are to *preserve* or *conserve* lovemaking and sexual intimacy for their marriage partner; unmarried people are to *reserve* these for expression inside the covenant of marriage. Proverbs specifically addresses men, but the Song of Solomon upholds the same value for women. Solomon praised his bride for her virginity (Song of Solomon 4:12–15), and the bride reflects on her decision to remain a virgin until marriage (Song of Solomon 8:8–10; see also chapter 7 in this book).

Since sin has distorted sexuality, human beings are easily lured away from the divine design. Though the attraction of illicit love may be powerful, such involvement brings catastrophic consequences. Consequently, explains Proverbs, reason must rule our passions. Casual sexual liaisons, which lack the depths of lifelong commitment and emotional intimacy, fall far short of true one-fleshness. They squander material, physical, and emotional resources, and bring the inevitable "reward" of regret. And ultimately, we must answer to God for our life choices.

The choice of lifelong faithfulness to God's design for sexuality in marriage is not only prudent, it also brings highly satisfying rewards. Proverbs uses the imagery of refreshing water in abundance as a delicate symbol that represents the sexual relationship between husband and wife. We should not disperse sexual energies in the streets, the wise man counsels. Rather, they are to be the source of lifelong delight and pleasure in the marriage union.

The phrase "the wife of your youth" implies that neither commitment nor sexual attraction need fade in old age. We had the honor of presenting a plaque of recognition to the couple married the longest in the United States; they were then celebrating eighty-five years of marriage. Local TV stations sent camera crews for interviews, and one reporter urged, "How about a kiss for the camera?" The husband eagerly obliged. Puckering up, he planted a big kiss on his wife's lips. Then, before letting her go, he asked, "You want more?" Without missing a beat, she came right back: "Any time, any place!"

This is what Proverbs means. Romance is to keep pace with aging. A husband is always to be ravished ("intoxicated," NKJV margin) by his wife's charms (Proverbs 5:18, 19). God's plan for sexuality not only protects people from pain, it withholds nothing good. He wants to make sure we know that sex in any other arena can't compare with sex in marriage. There aren't superlatives enough to describe it!

Child care in Proverbs

Proverbs is also concerned about child discipline: "Do not withhold discipline from a child" (Proverbs 23:13). Parents too often discipline children to punish them for disobedience or because they've been embarrassed by their children's socially unacceptable behavior. From Proverbs' perspective, parents should discipline to spare their children from the long-term, irreversible effects of wrong choices and habits. They should administer discipline in hope for the future (Proverbs 19:18).

From our vantage point in Christ, we understand discipline to be corrective, not punitive. God's admonition to discipline our children is not permission to use parental power and authority harshly or to relieve our own frustration. It is the process whereby loving parents—recognizing the strength of the sinful bent in human nature—guide their children's footsteps toward humanity's only help, Jesus Christ.[4] Discipline that is both kind and firm helps children grapple with their sinful natures and choose behaviors that demonstrate appropriate respect for themselves and others, enabling them to participate effectively in community. Effective discipline goes even further; it enlists the children's will on the side of growth and helps them mature.

In 2003, the remnants of Hurricane Isabel passed directly over our home. When the tropical-storm-force winds abated, we found all our trees intact except one, a ten-foot-tall pine. It was still rooted, but at the base of its trunk, it was bent at a right angle to the ground. Not wanting to lose the tree, we hauled it upright with ropes and staked it firmly in place. Amazingly, though a few needles dropped, the tree survived. The stakes are still there, and we'll keep them there until new growth enables the tree to stand tall against the wind once again. Just so, parents should seek to guide and correct their children through their formative years, until the children are mature enough to take adult responsibility.

The few verses in Proverbs (13:24; 22:15; 23:13, 14; 29:15) that mention the "rod" of discipline have received a lot of attention. Some references seem to use the word figuratively to refer to decisive discipline, such as the hard consequences Solomon reaped (Proverbs 22:15; 29:15; cp. 2 Samuel 7:14; 1 Kings 11:2, 4, 6). Popular within Christian parenting literature is the notion that the parental use of the rod should be like that of the heavenly Shepherd, who uses it to guide and comfort His flock (Psalm 23:4).[5]

Ellen White sheds this light on these passages: "Whipping may be necessary when other resorts fail, yet she [the mother] should not use the rod if it is possible to avoid doing so. But if milder measures prove insufficient, punishment that will bring the child to its senses should in love be administered. Frequently one such correction will be enough for a lifetime, to show the child that he does not hold the lines of control."[6]

Elsewhere, Scripture encourages parents to use patient teaching, consistent modeling, good communication, and warm relationships to influence change in children. Parents can communicate loving concern and the need for change verbally through conversation, a letter, or perhaps a story (see Psalm 39:11; Luke 17:2; cp. 2 Samuel 12:1–6). Very often, children are best corrected through experiencing the consequences of their choices (Luke 15:11–32). These are consistent with the wider approach of Proverbs that offers illustrations, appeals to logic and reasoning, and explains both the spiritual and everyday-life consequences of misbehavior. Always, parents must communicate their love to their children if they wish their discipline to be effective (Proverbs 13:24).

Almost everyone knows the proverb "Train a child in the way he should go, and when he is old he will not turn from it" (Proverbs 22:6). Less well known is the fact that the Hebrew word translated "train" has the nuance of "accustom." It is related to an old Arabic word for "initiate" that was used to describe how a midwife helped a newborn learn to suckle its mother's breast. She stimulated the sucking response by rubbing the baby's gums with the juice of something sweet, like stewed dates. In other words, Proverbs encourages parents to help children and adolescents stay on the way of life by whetting their appetites for godly values, by making these values so attractive and alluring that they are almost irresistible.

A verse like Proverbs 22:6 leaves some parents feeling anxious or guilty. It's all too easy to assume a linear relationship between good parenting and adult children who follow the ways of God. Similarly, it's easy to conclude that somehow parents are to blame when a child loses spiritual interest or rebels against parental values. However, if there is one thing Proverbs emphasizes, it is a person's power of choice. Proverbs provides *probabilities* rather than *promises.* God didn't intend Proverbs 22:6 to imply that children will *always* make choices in line with their upbringing. Rather than taxing parents with the impossible weight of moral responsibility for their children's ultimate destiny (a responsibility that belongs to the adult child), this proverb conveys the *likelihood* that positive attitudes toward God and spiritual things developed in childhood will linger into maturity.

Marry into real wealth

The theme of making wise choices continues through the wise man's concluding piece on choosing a marriage partner. Marriage, he declares, is a good thing (Proverbs 18:22), and nothing is of more value than a partner of noble character. Proverbs 31 plays on the word "virtuous" (KJV), also translated "noble" (NIV) and "rich" (cp. Psalm 62:10). Boaz uses this same word to affirm Ruth (Ruth 3:11). Perhaps the Moabitess, whose commitment and trust befits her place in the covenant line, provided the model for this poetic portrait. The wise man believed that real wealth lies in honorable character and fear of the Lord. There are no precious stones worth the price of a partner who has these characteristics.

A poetic device obscured by many translations provides a key to the interpretation of this passage. Each verse in Proverbs 31:10–31 uses one of the twenty-two letters of the Hebrew alphabet—the point being that the whole alphabet barely provides a sufficient framework to extol adequately the riches of godly wives! Rolled compositely into this portrait of one woman are the varied interests and skills of many: clothing manufacture, real estate, agriculture, home and financial management—her family can't say enough good about her!

Proverbs does not limit women's endeavors outside the home because of their gender. Were this chapter written today, think what else it might say: "She cares compassionately for her patients"; "She explores space"; "She serves her country in the military"; "She directs a Fortune 500 company." At the same time, this chapter does not diminish in any way wives and mothers who choose to concentrate their energies on the home front. The broad array of talent described here certainly does not require women to take on supermom multitasking in order to be counted among the virtuous. The description is not a checklist for a performance evaluation either by wives themselves or by their husbands. Rather, Proverbs calls us all to the character qualities that characterize godly marriage partners: trustworthiness, compassion, reliability, faithfulness, kindness, and industry.

The final verses of Proverbs offer a commentary on what is most important in life. Now as then, physical beauty often overshadows everything else. But, says the wise man, "Charm is deceptive, and beauty is fleeting" (Proverbs 31:30). Proverbs would free both women and men from the beauty myth, from the obsession with physical perfection that permeates the mind and traps humankind in a web of efforts to reach an impossible standard.[7] Thus, Proverbs ends where it began. If you would be truly wise, put your trust in the Lord and follow Him wherever He leads. The capstone quality of nobility for both men and women, wives and husbands, is the fear of the Lord.

1. Kenneth T. Aitken, *Proverbs* (Philadelphia, Penn.: The Westminster Press, 1986), 37.

2. Charles Wesley, "Jesus, Lover of My Soul," *The Seventh-day Adventist Hymnal* (Hagerstown, Md.: Review and Herald), 1985.

3. Ellen G. White, *Steps to Christ* (Nampa, Idaho: Pacific Press®, 1956), 72.

4. Ellen G. White, *Education* (Nampa, Idaho: Pacific Press®, 1952), 29.

5. Ann Eggebroten, "Sparing the Rod: Biblical Discipline and Parental Discipleship," *The Other Side*, April, 26–32, 1987, 23.

6. Ellen G. White, *Child Guidance* (Hagerstown, Md.: Review and Herald, 1954), 250.

7. See Naomi Wolf, *The Beauty Myth: How Images of Beauty Are Used Against Women* (New York: Anchor Books, 1992).

Invitation
to Intimacy

Sometime early in the tenth century A.D., Jewish intellectual Saadia ben Joseph, head of the rabbinic academy of Sura, Babylonia, sat down to prepare a commentary on the Song of Solomon. "You will find great differences in interpretation of the Song of Songs," he wrote in his introduction. "In truth they differ because the Song of Songs resembles locks to which the keys have been lost."[1] Saadia's opening remarks underscore a problem that has plagued this love poem for centuries, hampering its usefulness and obstructing the blessing God intended it to be.

Solomon's Song draws back the curtain on the intimate love life of a wedded couple, giving us glimpses of the allurement, the passion, the tenderness, and the exquisite delights they find in each other.

"How beautiful you are, my darling!" he croons, "Oh, how beautiful! Your eyes behind your veil are doves" (Song of Solomon 4:1*).

"My lover is radiant and ruddy, outstanding among ten thousand," she gushes admiringly in response. "His head is purest gold; his hair is wavy and black as a raven. . . . His mouth is sweetness itself; he is altogether lovely. This is my lover, this my friend" (Song 5:10, 11, 16).

---

*Hereinafter, in references, simply "Song."

The two speak unabashedly of their sexual attraction, thinly veiling their passion with delicate language and suggestive symbols. Therein lies the problem. Many religious people through the ages have shunned the Song as if it were an X-rated movie. They have perceived it as too sexually explicit to risk discovery by the young and have considered it unfit for discussion in mixed company. But there it is, in the collection of sacred writings. What are we to do with it?

Distracted by dualism

From his vantage point, Rabbi Saadia could reflect on only some thirteen centuries of bewildering efforts in Judaism to understand the Song. The Jewish scholars didn't mine it for its rich lessons about love and intimacy in marriage. Rather, they sought escape from its sexual content by reinterpreting it allegorically as a history of God's dealings with Israel.

This kind of reinterpretation began as Jews living in Alexandria three centuries before Christ imbibed the intoxicating philosophy of Greek dualism. According to this view, human beings are composed of two opposing parts: matter and spirit. It is the goal of life to free the spirit from the contamination of earthly matter—namely, the sexual body and its lusts. Greek intellectuals resorted to allegory as a method of interpreting their own ancient literature so as to disguise the lustful passions of the Homeric gods, which contemporary Stoics found distasteful and embarrassing. In this milieu, the plain sense of the Song of Solomon, with its emphasis on sexual passion and intimacy, caused the Hellenistic Jewish scholars such discomfort that they too spawned an allegorical approach in an attempt to make the biblical text more acceptable.

For long years, scholars bypassed the simple, literal sense of the Song in a search for hidden meanings that they considered less offensive. For example, Rabbis Rashi and Ibn Ezra interpreted the verse, "My lover is to me a sachet of myrrh resting between my breasts" (Song 1:13), as a reference to the Shekinah glory between the cherubim that stood over the ark. They took "Dark am I, yet lovely" (Song 1:5) to mean that Israel was dark because of the golden calf, but lovely because God had given them the Ten

Commandments.[2] Over time, people came to think of the Song as a symbolic history of Israel.

Unfortunately, dualistic philosophy infiltrated Christian thinking too. Many Christians took up the allegorical method of interpreting the Song and applied it to Christ and His church. For instance, they interpreted the woman's breasts as symbols for the Old and New Testaments, with Christ being the sachet of myrrh between them. Origen reinterpreted "Dark am I, yet lovely" of believers—dark because of sin, but lovely through conversion.[3]

Christian scholars pressed on in this vein for nearly two millennia, shearing away the sexual explicitness of the Song until it was viewed solely as an expression of spiritual love without fleshly taint. They offered no authority for their conclusions. Their interpretations stood purely on the strength of their ingenious imaginations.[4*]

Certainly, there is room for comparison between the delights of marriage portrayed in King Solomon's royal love song and the intimate bond that the heavenly Bridegroom desires to have with His church and with every believer. The Bible itself uses this imagery (see Isaiah 54:5; Jeremiah 2:2; Matthew 9:15; 2 Corinthians 11:2). Metaphor, however, is not the same as allegory. In fact, if we hope to appreciate fully the analogy between human marriage and the divine-human bond, we must first understand what the subject of the poem actually is—a literal love relationship between a man and woman.

Though sexuality and marriage are creation gifts of God, they've fallen on hard times in this sinful world. So, we might expect that God would give His people an inside look at marriage by His design—some worthy example of human love and sexual intimacy that could help us grasp the meaning of naked-and-unashamed oneness as God intended it in the beginning. Such an example the Song provides. But marriage is also to be a special witness that each couple bears to God's love and to the unity humankind may find in Him. The Song of Songs calls couples back to Eden so that their marriages may be a living portrayal

---

*When we announced the publication of *Love Aflame* (Hagerstown, Md.: Review and Herald, 1992), our book on the Song of Solomon, a friend exclaimed, "Oh, that's about Christ and the church."

of the redemption of the marriage institution that we can experience in Christ.

Unlocking Solomon's Song

Once, during a marriage retreat, we referred to Ellen White's positive view on sexuality in marriage and quoted the familiar lines, "Only where Christ reigns can there be deep, true, unselfish love. Then soul will be knit with soul, and the two lives will blend in harmony. Angels of God will be guests in the home, and their holy vigils will hallow the marriage chamber."[5]

After explaining that "marriage chamber" is Ellen White's term for the couple's bedroom, we saw a young wife cup her hand over her mouth in shock and disbelief. "Now you've done it," her husband said. "She was just beginning to get comfortable with the idea, and now you've told her angels are watching!"

Beneath his vain attempt at humor lay real pain for this couple. They shared privately that the wife's mother had instilled in her the belief that sex was only for procreation and that godly couples would put away all sexual pleasure in preparation for Jesus' coming. She found the thought that a smiling Creator would send angels to shelter and bless a couple in their lovemaking incomprehensible. To her, "watching angels" raised the specter of a displeased Deity sending clandestine agents to record a couple's bad behavior in heaven's books.

If Christian families are to rise above the sexual taboos that swirl around us, if we are to communicate in healthy ways as couples and share godly values regarding sexuality with our children, we must be open to Scripture's teaching on sexuality. The Song of Solomon is consistent with the biblical view of the body and of sexuality. First, the Bible presents a holistic view of human beings, with no dichotomy between body and spirit.[6] A person is a "living being" consisting of "body" plus "breath of life" (Genesis 2:7). The psalmist regards worship as involving the totality of one's being (Psalms 63:1; 84:2). In the New Testament, the total person is the object of Christian sanctification; all that one is and has is set apart for the holy purposes God intended (1 Thessalonians 5:23). "Therefore," Paul concludes, "honor God with your body" (1 Corinthians 6:20).

Second, Scripture recognizes sexuality as an integral part of human life. The Creator Himself made human beings—male and female—sexual beings as His final "very good" work before His Sabbath rest (Genesis 1:26–2:2). The wise man encouraged his son to enjoy sexual delights with his wife freely (Proverbs 5:18, 19). And Paul highlighted the mutuality of the sexual relationship in marriage; each partner's body, he said, belongs to the other and they share with one another by common agreement (1 Corinthians 7:1–5). This positive view of maleness and femaleness as created by God and redeemed in Christ provides the key we need to appreciate the Song of Solomon. It can dispel what one author has called the "psychological aversion to the obvious" in interpreting the Song at its most primary level. And in the experience of each married couple, it can free husband and wife to enjoy marital intimacy to the full.

Song Notes

As a student of literature, I (Karen) used Cliff's Notes as review summaries of major literary works. Here are a few "Song Notes":

The elusive story line. The song has a story line, but it can be elusive. The writer, from his inspired vantage point, considers narrative detail less important to God's purposes than portrayal of the intimate dialogue and celebration of sexual lovemaking between husband and wife.

Commentators who take a literal rather than allegorical approach agree the story is uncomplicated: King Solomon falls in love with a beautiful woman from the Lebanese countryside; her name is "Shulamite" or "Shulamith." He takes her in a grand marriage processional from her country home to Jerusalem to become his bride. In their marriage, the lovers are "lifted from a merely physical attraction to a true and pure love,"[7] fitly representing God's original design for marriage as well as the imagery of God's love for His people.

Song symbols. By using similes and metaphors, the writer can describe the intimate relationship of husband and wife discreetly and delicately. His primary symbol for the wife is the *vineyard-garden,* and for the husband, the *gazelle.*

Shulamith speaks of neglecting her own vineyard (Song 1:6). The reference here is to herself. The vineyard metaphor is part of broader garden imagery, where the woman's body and person is portrayed as a paradise of fragrant flowers and plants, succulent fruits, and refreshing fountains to be enjoyed by her beloved (Song 4:12–5:1).

Shulamith likens Solomon to a gazelle (Song 2:9). He is a gentle antelope who "browses among the lilies" (Song 2:16)—that is, he takes delight in her and draws his emotional nurturance from her love. He is a caring, trustworthy companion with whom she can safely risk "naked and unashamed intimacy" in every aspect of her life.

Mirrored poetry. Hebrew poetry is characterized by its *parallelism,* or "thought rhyme." In other words, the poet states a thought and then repeats it, enlarging upon it or suggesting a contrasting thought in one or more additional lines. For example, note "leaping across the mountains, bounding over the hills" (Song 2:8); "his left arm is under my head, and his right arm embraces me" (Song 2:6; notice also the contrast between "wall" and "door" in Song 8:9).

Sometimes the poet arranged thoughts in a mirrorlike parallelism known as a *chiasm.* This free translation of Song of Solomon 2:14 showcases this unique poetic structure:

> show me your face,   a
>   let me hear your voice;   b
> for your voice is sweet.   b′
>   and your face is lovely. a′

The chiastic structure is like seeing a rainbow reflected in a lake. The same bands of color appear in the water as are in the sky, but in mirror reverse.

Significantly, analysis of the poetic structure of the Song reveals that the entire poem is an intricate chiasm. (See the appendix, "Chiastic Structure of the Song of Solomon.") As is often the case, the lines at the very center of the chiasm provide the key to understanding its theme. In the Song, two delicately crafted verses describe the consummation of the couple's love on their wedding night (Song 4:16; 5:1), with, in the original Hebrew, 111 lines of poetry appearing before these center lines and 111 lines following them.

Not for married people only

The Song of Solomon contains important concepts that can enhance personal well-being and improve all relationships.[8]

It is good to be female, good to be male. Humans are sexual beings. The Song affirms this maleness and femaleness as very good. The sexuality of all human beings, whether or not they marry, is manifested in their maleness or femaleness as well as in the person they become and the unique way they go about life. Margaret Clarkson, reflecting on sexuality and singleness, notes that while Christian singles are called to refrain from the genital expression of sexuality, "in every other way we are free to express it to the utmost. And that utmost has a broad scope."[9]

Friendships are important. In the Song, the man and woman are first of all friends. She calls him "my friend" (Song 5:16) and his term "my love" literally means "my dear friend" (Song 1:9, 15; 2:2, 10, 13, etc.). They spend time together, enjoying one another's minds and offering one another sincere compliments and gestures of love. They share openly their fears and concerns and treat each other with mutual respect. Rather than using manipulation or force, they communicate their needs and desires openly to one another, inviting the other to respond. Good friendship is like that. There is close connectedness, even as each person values and protects the other's freedom to choose and to be himself or herself.

We are not alone. Idyllic though parts of the poem may be, clearly, fallenness has tainted the world of Solomon and Shulamith. Both knew brokenness growing up—he in the polygamous household of his father, David; she likely reared by a single mom (her father is never mentioned), with brothers who were not always kind to her (Song 1:6). Shulamith's disturbing dreams (Song 3:1ff; 5:2ff) hint at relational distress in the marriage. Maybe there are differences between them. Perhaps, despite her longing for lifelong commitment, she senses that her husband's eye has already begun to wander. Through these slices of real life, God offers us "the encouragement of the Scriptures [that] we might have hope" (Romans 15:4). We are not alone, no matter what the crises we face.

Love lessons for marrieds

The Song of Solomon is a guidebook for enhancing romance. The lead characters reserve time and special places for lovemaking, whether in their bedchamber or nestled among birds and blossoms, verdant trees, and refreshing streams. Their senses tingle with anticipation. Each serves up to the other a bouquet of physical and emotional delights. They exchange a breathtaking array of compliments. Likely Solomon's "your nose is like the tower of Lebanon" will need some translation for today's wives, but somehow in context it worked, and Shulamith knew that she was loved. When two are smitten with love, pillow talk wends where it will!

The intimacies of romantic love are a gift from the Creator Himself to create a bond so strong that it can last a lifetime. As couples surrender to the workings of divine love in their hearts, the best love of which human beings are capable is "refined and purified, elevated and ennobled."[10] Go ahead. Read it for yourselves. Take the parts of Solomon and Shulamith. Feel your pulse quicken as you make their joys your own!

Commitment is a recurring theme in the Song of Solomon. "On the day of his wedding," Solomon's "heart rejoiced" (Song 3:11). A wedding ceremony affords recognition of the couple's commitment to each other by both families, the community of faith, and the society at large. Shulamith's expression "My beloved is mine, and I am his" (Song 2:16, NKJV) is reminiscent of the covenantal language of the first marriage ceremony in Eden: " 'This is now bone of my bones and flesh of my flesh' " (Genesis 2:23). In the loftiest language of love and commitment in the Song, Shulamith entreats her beloved:

> Place me like a seal over your heart,
> like a seal on your arm;
> for love is as strong as death,
> its jealousy unyielding as the grave.
> It burns like blazing fire,
> like a mighty flame.
> Many waters cannot quench love;
> rivers cannot wash it away (Song 8:6, 7).

"Mighty flame" may also be translated as "the very flame of the LORD" (NASB). While human love is prone to transience, the love of which Shulamith speaks is a spark from that original flame of the Lord of love. It can be ours if we will unclasp our hands to receive it as a gift of the Holy Spirit (Romans 5:5). Such love bonds husband and wife in a lasting union. It is to the safety and nurturance of this love that children are entrusted. It is this same self-giving love that binds believers together in the body of Christ. The call of the Song of Songs is to make this love an active force in all our relationships.

It may seem incongruous that a lady's man like Solomon could write a piece about commitment in marriage. We think, however, that Solomon likely wrote the Song in later years, when, like Samson, he returned to the Lord after squandering his God-given gift for emotional and psychological insights in a reckless life. In this poetry of his old age, he recalls what might have been and lets God work lasting blessing out of his personal tragedy.

The Song in a promiscuous world

As we write, NBC News has just released a new survey of the sexual behavior of thirteen- to sixteen-year-olds in the United States. Compiled from one thousand interviews with teenagers in late 2004, the poll revealed that most—73 percent—of these early teens have not been sexually intimate. Unfortunately, this means that 27 percent of them are sexually active, a statistic that led MSNBC to confirm what parents know already: They and their teens are dealing with "a newly promiscuous world."[11] It is not news that sexual values in society run counter to the biblical view. But the rise of sexually promiscuous behavior among early teens forcefully reminds us how urgent it is that parents and others communicate to the young the biblical principles regarding sexuality.

Just as Proverbs warns young *men* against sexual promiscuity (see the previous chapter), so the Song of Solomon seeks to persuade young *women* to reserve sexual activity for marriage. During Shulamith's childhood, her brothers wondered whether, after puberty, she would allow easy sexual access to herself—i.e., be like a "door"—or whether she would guard her sexual purity as a "wall" (Song 8:8–10). Both before and within marriage, Shulamith declared herself to be a "wall," keeping herself only for her husband.

That decision is basis for the "peace" (verse 10, NKJV) she knows with her husband.

The use of the word "peace" is a play on the root word—Hebrew, *shalom*—from which both their names spring. *Shalom* means both "peace" and "whole" or "complete." When Shulamith came to Solomon on her wedding night, she was whole. She gave herself to him intact in every sense, including her sexual self. Solomon affirms her on their wedding night for being "a garden locked up, . . . a spring enclosed, a sealed fountain" (Song 4:12). "Here, *a fountain sealed* and *a garden locked* speak of virginity. The couple, while approaching consummation of their love, still have not reached that level of intimacy."[12]

Shulamith also speaks a word of caution to the "daughters of Jerusalem" as she reflects on moments of physical intimacy with her husband: "Do not stir up nor awaken love until it pleases" (Song 2:7; 3:5; 8:4). The likely intent is, "Do not arouse the intense passion of love until the right time," or, as *The Bible in Basic English* says, "till it is ready." On God's timetable, the right time is within the covenant of marriage.

In the face of a powerful new sexual taboo against virginity taking hold among youth, much more is needed than preaching against sexual involvement outside of marriage. It's true that youth need information; but more importantly, they need to feel connected to family, church, school, and community. Connectedness is the best antidote to risky behavior. Research has demonstrated that the kids who are involved in fewer behaviors that threaten their short-term and long-term well-being are the ones whose parents relate to them warmly, know their friends, are available when they need someone to listen, expect to know where they are and what they are doing, and talk to them about significant issues like sexuality.[13]

We cannot hope that we or our young people will be spared the devastating effects of sin on human sexuality or experience God's good gift to the full apart from a vibrant spiritual experience. When Paul calls believers to "glorify God in your body" (1 Corinthians 6:20, NKJV), he is mindful that in Christ, sexuality as it was in Eden has been restored. Here and now, we can glorify God in our bodies only when we consider our sinful natures crucified with

Christ and ourselves alive and raised to heavenly places through faith in Him as resurrected Lord (Romans 6:11–13). Ultimately, only an understanding of who human beings are in Christ can provide the motivation and the power young and old alike need to live the new life to which God has called us. It is a high calling, but it is the only way to abundant life.

1. Marvin Pope, *Song of Songs* (New York: Doubleday, 1977), 89.

2. H. H. Rowley, "The Interpretation of the Song of Songs," *The Servant of the Lord and Other Essays on the Old Testament* (Oxford: Basil Blackwell & Mott Ltd., 1965), 200.

3. Ibid.

4. *The Seventh-day Adventist Bible Commentary* (Hagerstown, Md.: Review and Herald, 1953), 3:1116.

5. Ellen G. White, *The Adventist Home* (Hagerstown, Md.: Review and Herald, 1952), 94.

6. *An Affirmation of God's Gift of Sexuality,* General Conference of Seventh-day Adventists World Commission on Human Sexuality, October 1997; as reprinted in Karen and Ron Flowers, *Human Sexuality: Sharing the Wonder of God's Good Gift With Your Children* (Silver Spring, Md.: Department of Family Ministries, General Conference of Seventh-day Adventists, 2004), 5, 6.

7. Rowley, 212.

8. Adapted from Ron Flowers, "Singles and the Song of Solomon," *Adventist Review* (December 24, 1992), 16, 17.

9. Margaret Clarkson, *So You're Single!* (Wheaton, Ill.: Harold Shaw Publishers, 1978), 27.

10. White, 99.

11. "Nearly 3 in 10 young teens sexually active," retrieved January 19, 2005, from <http://www.msnbc.msn.com/id/6839072/print/1/displaymod/1098/>.

12. G. Lloyd Carr, *The Song of Solomon* (Downers Grove, Ill.: Inter-Varsity Press, 1984), 123.

13. M. D. Resnick, et al., "Protecting Adolescents From Harm: Findings From the National Longitudinal Study on Adolescent Health," *Journal of the American Medical Association,* October 1997, 823–832.

CHAPTER

It's About Love

Estrangement in families hurts. Whenever upheaval rocks a household, thrusting its members apart, shockwaves are launched that shake all in the vicinity. The reverberations often resound across generations, with children and grandchildren impacted by family troubles of which they may not even be aware.

Every family experiences garden-variety problems that can usually be quite readily resolved. Some face dire threats to their family relationships in the wake of crushing betrayals of trust like adultery, incest, and family violence. Others struggle for years with the fallout of resentment and bitterness: Brothers separated for a lifetime over perceived unfairness in the property distribution of their dead father's will. Children forbidden to speak to certain relatives because of vicious rumors a generation old. Family reunions brought to an abrupt end because a widowed mother remarries. Stony silence between father and daughter after he boycotts her wedding. Husband and wife sleeping apart—he accusing her of infidelity, she protesting innocence. Some of these tragedies are open to public view, with relatives, friends, and even fellow church members drawn into the fray. Others are cloaked in secrecy, the family silently enduring their pain behind a façade of normalcy.

We recall the day our sons bore the sad news home from school that the mom of one of their little classmates had left town, leaving him and his daddy behind. All she said was that she didn't want to be a mother or a wife anymore. She never came back. For those of us looking on, it was all so sudden, so unexpected, so antithetical to the picture-perfect family we thought we knew. The jolt shook the community of faith as well as the neighborhood. Even as relatives, friends, and neighbors offered their support to this family, tremors of anxiety coursed through them. If it could happen to that family, could it happen to us? There was much introspection as we each looked to our own household.

God is no stranger to fractured family circles. Scripture is replete with stories of family members who were fighting, scheming, disowning, deceiving, depriving, and even destroying each other. Think of the sad narratives of the murder of Abel by his brother Cain, the lifelong animosity between Jacob and Esau, the betrayal of Joseph by his brothers, Amnon's brutal violation of his sister Tamar, Absalom's conspiracy against his father David, and Jesus' anecdote of an elder son who wouldn't welcome a prodigal brother returned home. Scripture preserves these stories to help us see that family disruption today is but an extension of age-old family maladies. God's redemptive activity in Christ is directed to these very kinds of sins. Jesus' prayer encapsulates His desire for all such families: " 'That all of them may be one, Father, just as you are in me and I am in you. May they also be in us so that the world may believe that you have sent me' " (John 17:21).

What is it that holds a family together? What goes so very wrong that it can cause a family to scatter in fragments, like shards of rubber on a highway when tread flies off a truck tire? Is there hope that families so badly shattered can be restored, or is the children's rhyme true of families too: "All the king's horses and all the king's men couldn't put Humpty together again"?

The missing ingredient

Having grown up with the 4-H Club, Ron enjoys an evening at the county fair as much as anyone does. Because his dad kept horses, Ron always gravitates toward the horse-pulling contest. Individual teams of horses take turns trying to drag a flat, weighted sled the greatest distance.

The last time we watched, one pair of mighty draft horses seemed certain to win. However, to the onlookers' surprise, the overwhelming combined strength of this team was completely squandered as first one and then the other jerked at the load. Despite their driver's urging, they couldn't move the load far. Other teams fared better.

Then the smallest horses entered in the contest were hitched to the heavy stone-drag. A titter ran through the crowd: What could this diminutive team possibly do? The crowd fell silent as the driver clucked and the muscles of the horses' shoulders, backs, and legs grew taut as they tested the weight. The chains strained. Then, as if some unspoken cue passed between them, the horses pulled in unison, matching step to sure step. Slowly they hauled the sled forward. In a few seconds, the victory distance was theirs. The scene conveyed a powerful illustration of what unity can accomplish.

Of course, human beings are not animals. Family unity and harmony do not spring from habit and conditioning, but from the hearts of family members. So what is the heart ingredient that makes the difference?

A couple once asked to talk to us in a last-ditch effort to save their marriage. We quickly detected the absence of warmth and caring between them. They kept their appointments, but they did little of the reading and the practical "doables" to which they agreed at the end of each session. And the sought-after warmth never came. In its place there grew an ever more perceptible indifference—a malaise of callous coldness and insensitivity filling the void where kindness, understanding, and love should have been. We later learned that this couple had divorced.

Someone has said that the opposite of love is not hate, but indifference. Strange as it may seem, the presence of hatred in a relationship yields a more hopeful prognosis for growth than a diagnosis of indifference. The expression of even a strong negative emotion signals that attachment still exists. Indifference indicates that the relationship is running on empty.

Karen's brother Les is quite the gourmet cook. Everyone looks forward to his roasted garlic tomatoes at Christmastime. Last year, Karen had run out of extra-virgin olive oil, so Les tried to make do with what she had on hand. It soon became clear, however, that there's no substitute. In families, there's no making do without love. It's the only glue that stands a chance of putting "Humpty Dumpty" families back together again.

We're not thinking of romantic love, nor even the friendship kind of love, though both will be present in a healthy marriage. At the foundation of all love lies a caring attitude, a mind-set that accepts and respects every person. It is a love that moves people to celebrate together in the good times and, in times of distress, to provide strength, empathy, and support. Such love is like soil nutrients to a plant. When the nutrients are present, the plant thrives; when they are absent, the plant withers and eventually dies.

A fundamental human need

Years ago, a wise Christian child psychologist suggested an important question that is basic to understanding problematic behavior: "I wonder why he [or she] does that?" The question reflects her understanding that, often, inner needs drive outward behavior. In our dealings with one another in the family, this question encourages us to look beyond the problem to consider whether there is a fundamental human need that, if met, might go a long way toward correcting the misbehavior.

One day when I (Karen) was working as a volunteer at a nearby Christian school, a teacher showed me a note written by a small boy who had the reputation of being perpetually in trouble. Hardly a day passed, it seemed, when his desk wasn't pulled up by the teacher's to keep him on task, or when he didn't get into a fight on the playground. Some of the faculty pressed for strong disciplinary measures, perceiving his naughtiness as a challenge to authority that demanded a firm response. Others agreed that misbehavior must come with consequences, but that it reflected problems in the family that were affecting the boy.

The teacher told me that after one particularly exasperating day, she was praying for her students. As she called up the little boy's face in her mind, she saw the sadness in his eyes as never before. She made a decision that night to try to think of him not as a bad little boy who made her job difficult but as a hurting little boy with more worries than a child should have to bear. While she continued to expect him to follow classroom rules, she made a special effort to smile at him often, to give him a hug whenever she got the chance, and to affirm him for everything she could find to approve. One day after she had begun making these efforts, he left a note on her desk.

Printed in a child's uneven hand, it read simply, "Dear Teacher, Thank you for loving me when I gots troubles. I gots so much troubles. Love, Jon."

It is true that sin has filled the human heart with selfishness. But there is another truth that can also help us understand the human condition and the behaviors that arise from this heart-sickness. This truth recognizes more than the selfishness that fills the fallen human heart. It perceives that the sin-sick heart is also empty, drained of the love for which it yearns because the connection with God who is Love is broken. As much as the heart needs to be emptied of selfishness, it needs to be filled with love.

Difficult people tend to bring out the worst in us. Their unpleasant qualities easily prompt reactions of cold silence, anger, and retaliation. We want to change them, so we lecture, argue, threaten, punish, ignore, or even cut off relationships all together. But Jesus sees beyond their unloveliness to the emptiness of their hearts. The words of the prophet Samuel describe Him well: " 'Man looks at the outward appearance, but the LORD looks at the heart' " (1 Samuel 16:7). Jesus saw people as "bruised reeds" bent to the point of breaking in the wind, and "smoldering wicks" with the ember of life nearly snuffed out (Matthew 12:20). Rather than destroying the reeds and extinguishing the wicks, He sought to bind them up and to fan the flickering flame back to life again.

Jesus' love proved to be a most powerful change agent. It rescued the fickle Peter from despair and transformed him into a steadfast leader. It inspired the no-longer promiscuous Mary to mingle costly perfume with her tears in gratitude. It changed the contentious, power-hungry John into a gentle pastor who could write, "Dear friends, since God so loved us, we also ought to love one another" (1 John 4:11). No less today, we need what Teresa Whitehurst has called Jesus' "heartseeing" vision—His capacity to see beyond frustrating behavior to the fundamental human need for love.

Agapē is the kind of love Jesus willed for us in His prayer. Such love is the essence of God's very nature (1 John 4:8). It is a radically different love from any that human beings can generate on their own. This high and lofty love toward which we stretch has the following qualities:

Unconditional. God's love is spontaneous. It flows from Him unconditionally, irrespective of human goodness and worth. The natural human heart offers love in exchange for something it wants. This love is conditional, dependent on returns, always attached to an "if." Paul captured the contrast when he wrote, "For a good man someone might possibly dare to die. But God demonstrates his own love for us in this: While we were still sinners, Christ died for us" (Romans 5:7, 8; cp. Ephesians 2:4–9).

Unchangeable. God's love is everlasting, unfailing, and constant (John 12:1; Romans 8:35–39; 1 Corinthians 13:8), while the affections of the human heart are changeable, fluctuating, and unreliable. Human love inevitably breaks down when severely tested. At the Last Supper, Peter declared his love for Jesus: "I am ready to go with you to prison and to death." Hours later, his love failed under the strain of accusation and fear (Luke 22:33, 57–62).

Self-giving. God's love gives, serves, benefits, and uplifts others (John 3:16; 1 Corinthians 13:5). "This is how we know what love is: Jesus Christ laid down his life for us" (1 John 3:16). Human love is preoccupied with self, primarily concerned with self-interest (Philippians 2:21; 2 Timothy 3:2; 1 John 2:15, 16). Jesus' parable of the praying Pharisee plainly unmasked this fatal human flaw: " 'The Pharisee stood up and prayed about himself: "God, I thank you that I am not like other men—robbers, evildoers, adulterers— or even like this tax collector. I fast twice a week and give a tenth of all I get" ' " (Luke 18:11, 12).

Jesus: love embodied

John 3:16 is the gospel in a nutshell: " 'God so loved the world that he gave his one and only Son, that whoever believes in him shall not perish but have eternal life.' " The universe stood in awe as God reached out with agape love to a rebel world. Then, in the grandest finale ever, God presented Himself—the very embodiment of this love—in human flesh so that we might know Him as He is.

The Gospels record the story of Love walking in our midst. We follow Him through the testimony of real people like ourselves who felt Love's touch. We witness the gruesome pain and agony Love bore for us, the anguish suffered as Love became the object of God's curse—all for love. We stand by John at the foot of the cross and hear the echo of Christ's words: " 'Greater love has no one than this, that he lay down his life for his friends' " (John 15:13). Ellen White spoke for Christians of all times when she wrote, "When you appreciate His wondrous love, love and gratitude will be in your heart as a wellspring of joy."[1] It is hard to imagine any other response.

The life and death of Christ are, however, more than simply an awesome display of love. "God was reconciling the world to himself in Christ, not counting men's sins against them" (2 Corinthians 5:19). Christ brought a change in the status of humankind before God. From the first announcement of His birth, the good news rang out. In Him, a state of peace is restored between earth and heaven. God's favor once again rests on humankind. At the Jordan, God Himself spoke: "This is My beloved Son, in whom I am well pleased." With Christ as our Representative, we are all God's sons and daughters in whom He is well pleased. Christ moved humankind from condemnation to justification (Romans 5:18). God has done everything He could do for our salvation. The call of the gospel is to accept this reconciliation and be at peace with Him (Romans 5:1; 2 Corinthians 5:20; Colossians 1:21–23).

But the good news doesn't end there. Paul goes on to declare that through Christ's crucifixion, all humanity has been reconciled to one another (Ephesians 2:13–16). Peace and oneness among all peoples, including our families, have become spiritual realities in Christ. "God *made* reconciliation. . . . In God's eternal purpose the death of Christ brought the death of alienation—not only between God and man but between man and man."[2] "Because we are one with God, we are also one with each other."[3] God calls us to make that spiritual reality our own and to walk in that oneness by living together according to the principles of Christ's kingdom.

In his monumental work *The Cost of Discipleship,* Dietrich Bonhoeffer shows how Christ stands between us as our great Center: "Since the coming of Christ, his followers have no more immediate realities of their own, not in their family relationships . . . nor in the relationships formed in the process of living. Between father and son, husband and wife . . . stands Christ the Mediator, whether they are able to recognize him or not. We cannot establish direct contact outside ourselves except through him, through his word, and through our following of him."[4]

A wonderful new spiritual reality exists; Jesus Himself connects us. We are like spokes on a wheel with Him as the hub. We can come together and find community only in Him—as a family, as a church, as a global village. We do not put Christ in His central position; we can only acknowledge it, follow Him, and reap the blessings of unity that come from the station He holds as our Mediator, on earth as well as in heaven.

The fruits of love

Love is the hallmark that distinguishes Jesus' followers (John 13:35). This love does not spring naturally from ourselves but will flood our hearts as Jesus abides there through His Spirit. He prayed that it might be so—" 'that the love you have for me may be in them and that I myself may be in them' " (John 17:26). And a braided cord of believers stands with Paul to testify to God's lavish response: "God has poured out his love into our hearts by the Holy Spirit, whom he has given us" (Romans 5:5). Christ's love in our hearts is the key to the love and unity that mark us as His disciples: "The cause of division and discord in families and in the church is separation from Christ. To come near to Christ is to come near to one another. The secret of true unity in the church and in the family is not diplomacy, not management, not a superhuman effort to overcome difficulties—though there will be much of this to do—but union with Christ. . . . The closer we come to Christ, the nearer we shall be to one another."[5]

The agape love of God in our hearts ushers in new attitudes of caring for others. We once knew a sister in one of our churches whose weekly petition at prayer meeting echoed the same refrain, "Lord, make us tolerant of one another." After we were members of that church for a while, we understood the utter urgency of her request of God. Behind the scenes lay a lot of narrow-mindedness and dissension.

But God's love calls us beyond tolerance. Paul, in fact, urges believers: "Be devoted to one another in brotherly love" (Romans 12:10)—literally, "with brotherly love to one another loving dearly." "Loving dearly" translates two root words, *philos* and *storgē,* which typically describe fondness and affection in families and close relationships. In effect, Paul was saying, "Be fond of one another; *like* each other." That can surely be a challenge. But when Christian homes and congregations become settings where fondness and caring draw people together, others will seek their warmth and come in out of the cold.

When our sons came home from school that day bringing the sad news about the mother who abandoned her family, we sensed that unspoken worries might well lurk within them. So we wanted to do something that would signal our own commitment to stay together. That evening for family worship we took our then fifteen-year-old wedding photo album off the shelf and summoned our boys to sit with us on our sofa. With our arms around each other, we paged through it and smiled with them at the young couple and all the happenings depicted on the pages. And there, before our sons, we pledged ourselves to each other again.

"How wonderful, how beautiful, when brothers and sisters get along!" wrote the psalmist (Psalm 133:1, TM). God's love can make it happen. With His love in our hearts, we can live the love we promise.

1. Ellen G. White, *Fundamentals of Christian Education* (Hagerstown, Md.: Review and Herald, 1923), 304.

2. Robert S. Folkenberg, "Diversity and the Divine Experiment," in Delbert Baker, ed., *Make Us One* (Nampa, Idaho: Pacific Press, 1995), 19.

3. Caleb Rosado, "Challenges of Change and the Church Mission," in Baker, 46.

4. Dietrich Bonhoeffer, *The Cost of Discipleship* (New York: The Macmillan Company, 1963), 108.

5. Ellen G. White, *The Adventist Home* (Hagerstown, Md.: Review and Herald, 1952), 179.

Seesaw Ride

The old wooden seesaw on our school playground broke when I (Ron) was in fourth grade. Taking care of our one-room rural school was a community concern, so one summer weekend, my farmer-builder father beckoned me to come along as he loaded lumber and tools on his farm truck and drove to the school. There he stripped away the remnants of the rotted seesaw—our "teeter-totter" as we called it—and built a new one. Some leftover red barn paint provided the finishing touch. When school reopened, I was there early and proudly presented the shiny new teeter-totter. All the students raced out at recess to get their turns on the new ride.

For a while, things went well, with friends balancing one another, gliding smoothly up and down. Then something changed. More kids wanted in on the action; they began hopping on by twos and threes. Soon it became a matter of seeing which side could keep the other up the longest. Eventually, boys tricked girls into riding opposite them and then dangled them, screaming, in mid-air. We little boys watched with, I'm sad to say now, considerable amusement.

Then one recess, it happened to me. While I was riding on the seesaw, some fifth-grade boys pushed my friend off the other end and got on. Instantly I was jerked into the air and held there, bouncing. It was scary. "Do you want down?" they jeered after a while. "OK, you're down!" With that, they hopped off and I crashed hard.

After that, I avoided the seesaw for a long time. The toy that was capable of bringing so much joy had become a place of pain.

Close relationships are a lot like a seesaw ride. As each of us mounts the relational seesaw with another family member, friend, or fellow believer, our personal characteristics, such as temperament, emotional well-being, and social status, combine to constitute the "weight"—the personal power we exert. The way we use our weight affects our experience and that of our partners.

Just as thoughtful seesaw riders adjust themselves to achieve balance and rhythm, so family members who have goodwill and warm regard for one another can work through their differences and find satisfaction in their life together. God's presence in the midst of families enables the individual members to find ways to respect each other's individuality while functioning well and enjoying strong connections with one another. Healthy Christian relationships are marked not only by efforts to keep conflicts to a minimum, but also by the commitment to surmount—in ways that accord with the gospel—the difficulties that inevitably arise.

Without the Spirit of Christ, a relational seesaw loses its balance. Selfishness and lack of concern for others skews the ride. Those given more power by the society around them use that power to control others for their own interests. Some who don't feel very valuable or secure may try to build themselves up by putting others down. Sometimes family members, like children on the playground, "pile on" to form alliances against one or more individuals in a family, until the seesaw tilts their way. Or family members who are self-absorbed and completely insensitive to the needs and well-being of their kin exert their power through abuse and aggression. Abusive behavior is the conscious choice of a person to control and dominate another. Unthinkable as it is, research reveals that the home is the single most violent place in society. Perpetrators of abuse and family violence make the seesaw ride a ride of terror. Their behavior is a distortion and perversion of love, for "love does no harm" (Romans 13:10).

Seesaw struggles

The behaviors in which people engage when they feel like the lightweights in a relationship or when they seek relief from people bent on abusing relational power to control others give evidence of remnants of God's creation intent for equality and mutuality in human relationships. Some instinctive sense of justice compels us to bring the relational seesaw into balance. But sinful and broken as we are, we often don't manage very well. Imbalance in the relationship, whether real or perceived, rarely leaves us content to just even up the power. As others have gone "one up" on us, so we determine to do whatever it takes to assume a position of power over them. Matilda is a good example:

> Doug was a dominating husband and father and ordered his family about as if he were a military commander. His wife, Matilda, had her own way of dealing with him. One day, for example, he was in a particular rush for them to go someplace in the car. He went out to the garage, started the engine, and backed the car out onto the driveway. It was his way of demanding that she hurry.
>
> When Matilda didn't come, he blew several long blasts on the horn. She heard the horn, but instead of joining him, detoured to the backyard and leisurely inspected her rose garden, plucking a few weeds, sniffing the fragrance of a few of the emerging blossoms. She made her way to the car in her own good time.[1]

The New Testament teaches believers the important social principle of *mutuality*—the outworking of love through reciprocal respect and shared responsibility in relationships. "Submit to one another out of reverence for Christ," Paul wrote (Ephesians 5:21). He presented this radical concept, found also in the teaching of Jesus and elsewhere in Scripture (see Matthew 20:26–28; Philippians 2:3–5; 1 Peter 5:5), as a characteristic of Christian believers who are filled with the Spirit (Ephesians 5:18). "Submit" (from the Greek *hupotassō,* "to put in place under") means "submission in the sense of voluntary yielding in love."[2] Reverence for Christ is the motivation that stimulates such a response. As E. K. Simpson says of Ephesians 5:21 in his classic commentary, "Self-seeking has been displaced by a nobler affection."[3] The phrase "to one another" implies that God intends for all believers to submit to one another; the submission is mutual. It is God's love at work, counteracting the natural selfishness that motivates people to dominate and exert power over others.

In the days of early mission work in the South Pacific, pastor-evangelist John Fulton worked in Fiji, where he baptized Ratu Ambrose, one of the island nation's powerful chieftains. Ambrose was known far and wide for his cruel treatment of his subjects. To launch his heavy war canoe he would conscript men from among his subjects, bind them, and use them as human logs or rollers. Many died; others were left with scarred and broken bodies.

As Pastor Fulton conducted the first foot-washing service after Ambrose's baptism, the old chief was quick to respond to the pastor's instruction. He took the towel and basin across the room and knelt before another new church member, a crippled man named Matui. It turns out that Matui had been maimed as one of the human logs under Ambrose's great canoe. "It is not right for you to wash my feet," protested Matui. "You are a great chief, and I am only a fisherman."

Bending humbly before the broken fisherman, tenderly holding his feet in his hands, Ambrose replied, "There is only one Chief here in this room tonight, and that is Jesus." Ambrose's response was the surest evidence the gospel of Christ had done its work in his heart.

Submission at home

The apostle Paul realized that if members of the smallest church—the household—understood and practiced mutual submission, it would transform the larger fellowship of faith. So he immediately made application of the principle to three pairs of domestic relationships—that of wife and husband, child and parent, and slave and master (Ephesians 5:22–6:9). The counsel he gave to all three pairs of relationships falls under the umbrella of Ephesians 5:21. Exegesis of the passage and the connection between verses 21 and 22 reveal that submission is not the duty of the wife alone, as has often been taught. The mutual-submission principle extends to all.

Paul explained Christian submission first to the socially weaker side of each pair. His intent was not to reinforce the existing social order, which required the subjection of those with lesser status—wives, children, and slaves—to those to whom society gave greater power—husbands, parents, and masters. Rather, Paul sought to show that because old distinctions have been done away with in Christ (Ephesians 2:13–18) and we all are one in Him (Galatians 3:28), the faith culture of Christ introduces a radically different approach to relationships from the domination/subjection way of the world.

In addressing the socially weaker groups, Paul consistently used a qualifier that makes an important distinction between submission as Christians and the subjection common to the culture. For wives, their submission is "as to the Lord" (Ephesians 5:22); for children, it is "in the Lord" (Ephesians 6:1); and for servants, "as to Christ" (Ephesians 6:5).

Paul addresses next those with greater social power (husbands, parents, and masters), giving them directives regarding their submission that were also radically different from cultural norms. Husbands are to love their wives with God's self-sacrificing agape love (Ephesians 5:25, 28). Parents are to turn from harsh parenting practices to a nurturing style (Ephesians 6:4). Masters are to demonstrate the care and impartiality of God to servants (Ephesians 6:9).

This teaching must have astonished believers in the first century. It may be equally surprising to us. But it demonstrates in practical terms the level ground on which human beings stand at the foot of the cross. With God, there is no elevation of one over another (Ephesians 6:9). Just as children make themselves vulnerable to a partner riding on a seesaw, so Christians voluntarily submit themselves to one another in close relationships. Such submission "is one way of letting the mind of Christ be revealed in human relationships."[4]

Sometimes good Christians think they should not resist when someone takes advantage of them or stand up for themselves when they are oppressed. For instance, we know of husbands who have taken advantage of their wives—making sexual demands, restricting their input into decision making, and limiting their contacts and involvement outside the home—and then have equated such "submission" with spirituality.

The concept of submission has also become entangled with the biblical perspective on the meaning of suffering in the life of a Christian. People have produced devastating results by applying Peter's comment "If you suffer for doing good and you endure it, this is commendable before God" (1 Peter 2:20; see 1 Peter 4:12–

19) to situations in which there was abuse within families. James and Phyllis Alsdurf cite cases where women have endured abuse because of a faulty understanding of suffering and submission, particularly as husbands and pastors have misinterpreted submission as applying only to wives.[5] First Peter, however, was written to a very particular circumstance—the membership of the church was composed of a high percentage of slaves. So Peter extended some consolation, some positive reframing of suffering, to persons for whom there was no other option except to bear it.

Biblical submission does not negate the worth, dignity, and respect due every human being by virtue of creation and redemption. Submission promotes a balance of power that leads to unity and peace. But that unity springs from Christ's presence in the heart and from the knowledge that in Him we died to old ways of living and rose to a new life. The appeal to "hierarchy" or "chain of command" in the family or in the church is a worldly method of bringing about order—one that perceives power, control, and fear as the only way to create any semblance of unity and peace.

Philippians 2:3 says, "Do nothing out of selfish ambition or vain conceit, but in humility consider others better than yourselves." We might have misunderstood this verse had the apostle not followed it with the carefully worded corollary principle to submission enunciated in verse 4: "Each of you should look not only to your own interests, but also to the interests of others." Verse 4 explains that verse 3 does not mean the neglect of one's own vital interests as a Christian person. To the contrary, it presents the balance so important to Christian relationships. We can think of it in terms of our seesaw metaphor, with "your own interests" on one end and "the interests of others" on the other. The "but also" in the middle acts as a fulcrum on which the two are balanced. In the Christian life, both are to receive appropriate attention. Human nature is self-centered, filled with self-ambition; it is not by nature other-centered. However, there is an appropriate self-care that is not selfish.[6]

Philippians 2:3 combats selfish ambition, and then verse 4 helps believers avoid the traps of codependency and overinvestment in others that can lead to dysfunction and make them vulnerable to abuse. The mature Christian exhibits agape love toward God, toward fellow human beings, and toward self (see Matthew 22:39).

Enjoying the ride

For nearly three decades, we were members of a truly unique fellowship of believers. Capital Memorial Seventh-day Adventist Church, in Washington, D.C., has become a multinational Christian family, with members from some forty-five nations. If the truth be told, the congregation didn't always like the same foods nor enjoy the same music. Members wrestled hard with one another on church boards. But with dedicated and persistent Christ-centered pastoral leadership and a commitment to live by the biblical appeal, "Dear friends, since God so loved us, we also ought to love one another" (1 John 4:11), this diverse group became family.

A crowning moment came one Easter season when the church celebrated a Friday evening agape meal and Communion service. Around the candle-lit table of fellowship, members bore testimony to their love for Christ and their love for one another. One African brother, serving in the diplomatic corps from South Africa, had been a member of the church since rediscovering Adventism at a prayer breakfast held there for diplomats and their Adventist denominational leadership counterparts. As Ezra, so familiar with the policies and practices of apartheid, stood that evening, he glowed with an inner light that eclipsed the candles. We still remember his ecstatic comment: "That *thing* they speak about [that the gospel brings together red and yellow, black and white]—it's really working here!" The spirit at that Communion table was the work of God's grace in human hearts, bearing fruit in a fellowship founded on the practical teachings of the gospel regarding relationships.

Here are some specific things we can do as families that are important to bringing joy to our journey, to enjoying our ride in relationships.

Build one another up. "Encourage one another and build each other up" (1 Thessalonians 5:11). We are "the wind beneath the wings" of those we love. Our weight on the seesaw lifts up those with whom we are in relationship, building them up, giving them every opportunity and encouragement to become all that they can be.

Put anger in its place. Anger as an emotion is part of life in Christ. " 'In your anger do not sin': Do not let the sun go down while you are still angry" (Ephesians 4:26). Though angry attitudes and behaviors are destructive to individuals and relationships (Genesis 49:6, 7; Psalm 37:8; Matthew 5:22; Galatians 5:19–21), the feeling of anger is not sin. Jesus, who knew no sin, experienced this emotion (Mark 3:5).

Anger sounds a warning within us when we detect inequity, injustice, oppression, or unfair treatment of ourselves or others. We should address our anger promptly, reporting our emotion to the one with whom we have the issue, checking our perception, and processing our concerns as necessary. Final resolution may take time, but anger can often be diffused by a "soft answer" (Proverbs 15:1, KJV). "Soft answers" are caring responses that involve listening to and accepting the person while recognizing the deeper feelings like fear, frustration, or hurt that triggered the anger. Getting behind the anger in this way helps families clear things up and grow closer.

Make peace. "Let us therefore make every effort to do what leads to peace" (Romans 14:19). Love and tolerance enable many families to cope with great differences. If family members don't resolve problems, hostility and distance may develop in the relationship. Healthy conflict resolution includes open and honest communication between the persons involved (Matthew 18:15; Ephesians 4:25) as well as consideration of each other's perspectives and the needs that underlie each one's concerns (Philippians 2:4). Desire for mutuality beckons Christians to find win-win solutions.

Situations of abuse and family violence call for skilled intervention. Professional treatment can bring about change in abusers' behaviors, but only if the abusers take responsibility for their behaviors and, cooperating with such help, stop abusing others and allow God's agape love to heal their own hearts and enable them to love others (see Ephesians 3:20). Victims of violence in Christian families need support to find safety for themselves and their children and to meet other practical and emotional needs. Christian friends can also help by connecting victims with professional care and providing stability in times of unrest.

Forgive one another. Forgiveness is God's gift to families when hearts and relationships have been wounded. It is first of all a decision to let go of the destructive malice of revenge. We remind our wounded hearts that Christ has atoned for all sin. We pass forgiveness on, "forgiving each other, just as in Christ God forgave you" (Ephesians 4:32). The wounded one is freed within, whether or not the offender asks for forgiveness.

Forgiveness also has a second phase—one that's made possible when the wrongdoer repents (Luke 17:3, 4). Repentance opens the door for the wounded safely to consider reconciliation. True repentance always includes stopping the offending behavior, taking responsibility for the behavior and damage done, making sincere apology, making restitution in every way possible, and making changes to protect against reoccurrence.

Reconciliation in human relationships can come about in the lives of wounded ones and wrongdoers with God's help when both are willing to work at the hard task of rebuilding trust. Some relationships may be so broken that, though there is forgiveness, reconciliation is simply out of reach. Ultimately, we can stay on the seesaw only with those we trust and with whom we continue to build strong bonds.

In 1772, John Fawcett, the Baptist pastor of a little church in Yorkshire, England, accepted a call to a larger church in London. After his farewell sermon, people gathered around his family and tearfully begged them not to go.

"I can't take this," Fawcett's wife sobbed.

"Neither can I," he replied. "Unpack the wagons!"

Fawcett wrote the hymn "Blessed Be the Tie That Binds" to celebrate the ties of fellowship that held him.

Blest be the tie that binds our hearts in Christian love!
The fellowship of kindred minds is like to that above.
Before our Father's throne we pour our ardent prayers;
Our fears, our hopes, our aims are one, our comforts and our cares.
We share our mutual woes, our mutual burdens bear,
And often for each other flows the sympathizing tear.
When we asunder part, it gives us inward pain;
But we shall still be joined in heart, and hope to meet again.

---

1. Karen and Ron Flowers, *Love Aflame* (Hagerstown, Md.: Review and Herald, 1992), 17.

2. W. F. Arndt and F. W. Gingrich, *A Greek-English Lexicon of the New Testament and Other Early Christian Literature* (Chicago: The University of Chicago Press, 1979).

3. E. K. Simpson and F. F. Bruce, *Commentary on the Epistles to the Ephesians and the Colossians* (Grand Rapids, Mich.: Wm. B. Eerdmans Publishing Co., 1957), 127.

4. John C. Howell, *Equality and Submission in Marriage* (Nashville, Tenn.: Broadman Press, 1979), 58.

5. See James and Phyllis Alsdurf, *Battered into Submission* (Downers Grove, Ill.: InterVarsity Press, 1989).

6. See Ray S. Anderson, *Self Care* (Wheaton, Ill.: Victor Books, 1995).

CHAPTER

Passing on Jesus

Every four years, in advance of the Olympic Games, runners carry the emblematic lighted flame to the new site of the games. As a runner completes the prescribed distance, he or she hands the torch to the person who will run the next leg of the journey. Every generation of believers is like one of these runners. They each go their distance but eventually must pass the torch of faith to the next generation.

Moses considered passing the faith torch a family affair. In his parting words, he pressed upon Israel the importance of conveying the heritage of faith: " 'These commandments that I give you today are to be upon your hearts. Impress them on your children. . . . Be careful that you do not forget the LORD' " (Deuteronomy 6:6, 7, 12).

So, just what is the torch of faith we are to convey to our children? What will create the best likelihood that we can effectively hand it off to our children? How will we know when we have passed it successfully? These questions are some of the most important that parents—and the extended family and community of faith who support them—can ponder.

On many occasions, in many parts of the world, we have asked parents these questions. Responses have varied widely from "Christian values," through "love for God," "the Ten Commandments," "Adventism," "Bible teachings," to "the ability to think for themselves about faith and make their own decisions." We remember one group whose answer was simply, "Jesus." "We want to pass Jesus to our children," they said. "Jesus is the torch we want to convey to the next generation."

What an intriguing thought—passing a *Person* on to the next generation! The group's answer set us all to thinking about how central Jesus is to everything we believe. As we've reflected on that response, we've come to see what a full and complete answer it is—what a full and complete answer He is! Christ is the essential core of Christian faith and experience. Jesus Himself said, "Now this is eternal life: that they may know you, the only true God, and Jesus Christ, whom you have sent" (John 17:3). When people asked Him, "What must we do to do the works God requires?" His answer was simple and clear: "The work of God is this: to believe in the one he has sent" (John 6:28, 29).

It was this belief in Him, this faith in Him that Jesus sought in all His followers (Luke 8:25; Matthew 16:15). He rejoiced when anyone turned to Him in faith for help and healing: "When Jesus saw their faith, he said to the paralytic, 'Son, your sins are forgiven' " (Mark 2:5). Jesus' heart was especially moved by the faith demonstrated by those outside the covenant community, who had far less evidence on which to base faith than did those on the inside: "Jesus . . . said to those following him, 'I tell you the truth, I have not found anyone in Israel with such great faith.' . . . Then Jesus said to the centurion, 'Go! It will be done just as you believed it would.' And his servant was healed at that very hour" (Matthew 8:10, 13).

Jesus also knew all too well that people can express great conviction one day and lose it all the next. After He fed the multitude with the loaves and fishes, many among them conspired to take Him by force and proclaim Him the king of Israel.[1] He foiled their plan however, sending the disciples away in a boat and disbanding the crowd. When the crowd found Him again the next day, Jesus explained the spiritual nature of His kingdom—that it was not a kingdom of this temporal world, but a kingdom made real through faith in Him. John made this sad comment about that day: "From this time many of his disciples turned back and no longer followed him" (John 6:66). Jesus then asked the Twelve, "You do not want to leave too, do you?" Peter's response encapsulates the essence of Christian faith: "Lord, to whom shall we go? You have the words of eternal life. We believe and know that you are the Holy One of God" (John 6:67–69).

Jesus foresaw the assaults upon faith that the last days would bring. One can hear the longing in His heart when He asked a rhetorical question that echoes down through history: "When the Son of Man comes, will he find faith on the earth?" (Luke 18:8).

Faith through time

Despite the attempts of Moses and Joshua, his successor, to help successive generations of Israelites to hold on to their faith, Scripture records a disturbing reality. As time passed and the eyewitnesses to the Exodus from Egypt and settlement in Canaan died, Israelite commitment to the Lord faded. "They forsook the LORD, the God of their fathers" (Judges 2:12). Studies confirm that the founders of a church or organization demonstrate very high levels of commitment to the beliefs and values espoused by the group. Usually, they were the ones who first championed them. Adventist pioneers were no exception. They knew exactly why they believed what they believed.

One of those leading pioneers was Joseph Bates, a whaling ship captain who lived in New Bedford, Massachusetts, in the 1840s. Early in our ministry, we served as a pastoral couple in the district that encompasses New Bedford. Bates's encounter with a fellow townsman on Fairhaven Bridge is a celebrated piece of Adventist lore that we often heard recounted with pride when we were there. Bates had just returned from a series of intense studies during which a Bible truth that would become a major tenet of Adventist doctrine was established.

"What's the news, Captain Bates?" a townsman called out in greeting as he spied Bates on the bridge.

"The news," replied Bates, "is that the seventh day is the Sabbath of the Lord!"

Captain Bates became a leading exponent of the Seventh-day Adventist faith. He had participated in the process of earnest Bible study and prayer that set the values of this young religious movement, and he had made those values his own.

The next generation to come along generally adopts the ideals of their elders largely because of the zealous teaching and role modeling of their parents. But by the following generation, many have begun to lose sight of the principles behind the values. They may conform, but often more out of habit than conviction. In subsequent generations, habit patterns tend either to break down or to crystallize into traditions whose meaning is largely lost. What was left of the founders' passion dissipates to nothing.

In one traditional approach to transmitting values, older people simply *tell* the youth what to believe. It's true that for many children, what will become personal faith begins as family faith. However, believing something because your parents believe it is not the same as developing personal faith. A person's faith becomes mature only when that person internalizes beliefs and values. Only then has the "torch" been passed—and until then, the faith of the fathers is in peril. As John Youngberg, professor of religious education at Andrews University, puts it so well: "Great ideals don't live on just because they are great or even because they are true. They live on only when they are enshrined in the hearts of the young. Our most treasured religious beliefs are always only one generation from extinction!"[2]

The parents who spoke of "passing on Jesus" to their youth were on to something vital. Knowing Jesus personally kindles excitement about His teachings and a passionate desire to know more, to follow Him wherever He leads, to be a part of the body of Christ. This is discipleship indeed. There's something far better than telling the next generation the exact dimensions of the doctrine they must hold. It is to help them discover Jesus for themselves, as their forebears did, through the revelation of His Word. We can trust that Jesus' Spirit will guide them into all truth just as He has us. When they've placed their hands in the hands of the Christ we love, we can safely release them into the future.

A few years ago, we helped to organize an international congress on youth evangelism in Prague. While preparing to lead a walking tour of this modern hub of the Czech Republic, once the ancient capital of Bohemia, we went looking for the Bethlehem Chapel of early Protestant Reformer John Huss fame. We wandered down medieval cobblestone streets toward the little sanctuary tucked amid shops and row houses. In our imaginations we were chapel-goers six centuries ago when this little place of worship was new and a freshly ordained priest known to the locals as Jan Hus, rector of the University of Prague, had just been appointed its minister. As we opened the weathered door and stepped over a worn threshold, we were transported back to an era when belief was put to an excruciating test and a man stood up against a storm that threatened the very foundations of Christendom.

In that little chapel, we visualized this great preacher proclaiming the powerful truths that would send rays of light across Europe, even as they led to his excommunication and martyrdom: "The precepts of Scripture, conveyed through the understanding, are to rule the conscience; in other words, that God speaking in the Bible, and not the church speaking through the priesthood, is the one infallible guide."[3] Later, in the Old Town, we gazed silently at the statue of Hus that dominates the city square, a memorial to a beloved pastor and religious reformer whom the papal Council of Constance condemned as a heretic and burned at the stake there in 1415. Just before Hus died, he expressed faith in the One he had come to know and believe: " 'I do commend my spirit into thy hands, O Lord Jesus, for thou hast redeemed me.' "[4]

The attraction of this age

One particular challenge to faith that confronts the families who would follow Jesus is that even as they are sojourners on earth awaiting their Lord's return, they are really citizens of heaven (John 14:3; Philippians 3:20). The New Testament writers speak of the peril to believers from the "world" (Greek *kosmos*) and from this "age" (Greek *aiōn*). The apostle John uses the term *kosmos* most often in this context: "Do not love the world or anything in the world" (1 John 2:15). Matthew, Mark, Luke, and Paul particularly use the word *aiōn*, sometimes also translated as "world" or "life." Paul's sad comment about the loss of his companion and assistant Demas is a poignant example: "Demas, because he loved this world, has deserted me" (2 Timothy 4:10). In this passage, "this world" is literally "this age."

Demas's desertion takes on significance when we comprehend more fully what John meant by "this world" and what Paul and other writers meant by "this age." Biblical writers often contrasted "of this world" with "not of this world" (John 8:23; 15:19; 18:36). They also contrasted "this age" with "the age to come" (see Matthew 12:32; Mark 10:30; Luke 18:29, 30). In one sense, both contrasting pairs divide human existence along a timeline. "This age" will end with the second coming of Christ. By implication, the "age to come" will begin then (Matthew 13:22). John wrote, "the world" is passing away (1 John 2:17). In Revelation, he envisioned the time when " 'the kingdom of the world has become the kingdom of our Lord' " (Revelation 11:15).

However, we don't fully explain the concepts of two worlds and two ages by plotting them on a timeline. They also represent two opposing realms. Satan is " 'the prince of this world' " (John 12:31; 14:30; 16:11), "the god of this age" (2 Corinthians 4:4). Christ and His kingdom are " 'not of this world' " (John 8:23; 18:36) but " 'from above' " (John 3:31; 8:23). The good news of the gospel is that the incarnation of Christ inaugurated "the age to come." While we await Christ's kingdom of glory, His kingdom of grace is now in our midst (Matthew 12:28; Luke 11:20; 17:21). Christ considers His followers "not of this world" (John 15:19; 17:14, 16). He has given "himself for our sins to rescue us from the present evil age, according to the will of our God and Father" (Galatians 1:4). Believers have experienced the power of the age to come (Hebrews 6:5).

Powerful engines lift airplanes aloft and keep them skimming the skies against the pull of gravity. Yet the earthward tug is relentless. A change in outside atmospheric pressure can cause a plane to drop hundreds of feet in seconds, leaving one's stomach fluttering from the free fall. Without power to offset gravity, all aircraft would eventually fall back to earth.

Like earth's gravitational force, "this world" and "this age" draw us to them. But Scripture is insistent that believers in Christ have what it takes to escape the gravitational pull of "this world." By the mighty power of God, Jesus ascended to heaven and escaped the forces of this world that tried to hold Him. By putting us into Christ (1 Corinthians 1:30), God has raised believers to and seated them in "the heavenly realms" (Ephesians 2:6ff). As Christians, we have a status that is beyond the reach of this world or this age. We have passed from death to life (John 5:24; 1 John 3:14), from condemnation to justification (Romans 5:15–21). Though we await release from the presence of sin, God has freed us from sin's penalty and power: "If the Son sets you free, you will be free indeed" (John 8:36; cp. Romans 6:14).

In the light of the truth of all that Christ's atonement has accomplished, God calls us to think of ourselves as He thinks of us: "Since, then, you have been raised with Christ, set your hearts on things above, where Christ is seated at the right hand of God. Set your minds on things above, not on earthly things. For you died, and your life is now hidden with Christ in God" (Colossians 3:1–3). "Count yourselves dead to sin but alive to God in Christ Jesus. Therefore do not let sin reign in your mortal body so that you obey its evil desires" (Romans 6:11, 12). One can hear sadness in Paul's voice as he lamented the loss of Demas. What Demas did was not the slip of a weak moment. It was a persistent, deliberate, ultimate choice to love this age more than the age to come. In so choosing, he turned his back on the most important Person of all. Demas chose not to believe in Jesus, not to accept his status "in heavenly realms in Christ." Because God will always respect our freedom to choose, the decision that can separate us forever from Life belongs to us alone.

Living within one's culture

Jesus told His Father, "My prayer is not that you take them out of the world but that you protect them from the evil one. They are not of the world, even as I am not of it" (John 17:15, 16). Each believer, each family, can take courage from Jesus' prayer. With Jesus praying for us, in view of His assertion that His followers are not of this world, with the assurance that God protects those who are His, we and our families can live holy lives in this world.

Though every culture mirrors the fallen condition of the people within it, each one also bears the imprint of the Creator. So, we can expect to find in every culture some beliefs and practices that Scripture affirms. Christians in such cultures can uphold and strengthen that which is good and in keeping with biblical principles. However, it is just as certain that Christians will have to discard some cultural beliefs and practices altogether and modify others that they wish to keep. Unfortunately, church history shows that some efforts to ac-commodate culture have yielded a patchwork of pseudo-Christian beliefs and practices that pose as authentic Christianity. Christians in every culture must use great care to avoid compromising truth.

While, as Christians, we must seek to avoid the contaminating aspects of the culture around us, Christ has sent us into the world to make disciples. His assurances that God has given Him all author-ity and that He will be with His followers to the end of the age seem specifically directed at empowering us to work for Him within our cultural settings (Matthew 28:19, 20). Through counseling with one another, studying God's Word, and prayer for guidance by His Spirit, we can discern what to discard and what to retain from soci-ety around us. We can also determine how best to salt and light the world. Christ and the apostles, our models, didn't confront culture directly. Rather, they worked change from heart to heart and home to home, one person and one family at a time.

The late Dr. E. C. Banks, longtime Adventist seminary professor, and his late wife, Letah, held many marriage seminars. At one of them, they introduced us to a large painting of Jesus walking on the water. Then, in their never-to-be-forgotten devotional, this older couple of long experience recounted the story of Jesus walking across the sea to aid His disciples, who were battling a crisis. Then the Bankses asked, "What does this picture say to you?"

Gazing on the canvas, people commented, "His face is so calm and reassuring!" "He knows no fear." "His feet are completely dry." "His extended hands invite us to walk on the water with Him." Many a troubled couple reported that this simple exercise of reflec-tion on Jesus' mastery of the elements renewed their personal faith in Him as Lord of all and supplied them with fresh courage to face change and difficulty.

Ellen White painted her own picture of how to live vibrantly as families of faith in such a way that the next generation will hardly be able to resist making our faith their own:

> When Christ took human nature upon Him, He bound humanity to Himself by a tie of love that can never be bro-ken by any power save the choice of man himself. Satan will constantly present allurements to induce us to break this

tie—to choose to separate ourselves from Christ. Here is where we need to watch, to strive, to pray, that nothing may entice us to choose another master; for we are always free to do this. But let us keep our eyes fixed upon Christ, and He will preserve us. Looking unto Jesus, we are safe. Nothing can pluck us out of His hand.[5]

1. Ellen G. White, *The Desire of Ages* (Nampa, Idaho: Pacific Press®, 1940), 378.

2. John B. Youngberg, *Deuteronomy 6: Clearest Biblical Charter for Religious Education* (Berrien Springs, Mich.: Department of Religious Education and Educational Foundations, Andrews University, 1991), 3.

3. James. A. Wylie, *The History of Protestantism* (New York: Cassell & Company, Limited), Book 3, Chapter 2, as quoted in Ellen G. White, *The Great Controversy* (Nampa, Idaho: Pacific Press®, 1988), 102.

4. White, *The Great Controversy,* 109.

5. Ellen G. White, *Steps to Christ* (Nampa, Idaho: Pacific Press®, 1956), 72.

Contagious Homes

The house appeared first as a soft ruby glow, indistinct through the leafless oaks of December. Cars crawled by slowly in both directions—block-long processions drawn through this quiet neighborhood in Washington, D.C., by the news that, again this year, the family had followed their tradition. "Be sure you see it," church members had told us. "It's unforgettable." So, we joined the line, curious to view this unusual sight.

We inched forward until we were squarely in front of the house, and then we paused to drink in the picture. Thousands of miniature red bulbs outlined the exquisite features of the grand Tudor architecture; every detail of the house was perfectly reproduced in lights, down to the last pane of window glass. Neat rows of the same miniature red lights trimmed the boundaries of the lawns, walks, and gardens, while even more red played hide-and-seek among the hedges. Prominent on the front lawn was a life-size Nativity scene bathed in pure white. The figures were carefully set so that passersby could see the faces of Mary and Joseph gazing transfixed on the infant Jesus in the manger. The shimmering crèche against the crimson backdrop provided a truly awe-inspiring Christmas greeting.

The myriad points of light around the Bethlehem stable drew all eyes to contemplate the most singular event in human history— the coming of God into the world in the person of His Son. For more than two decades, this December display had a magnetlike effect upon the northwest corner of the city. Perhaps this family had decided that in an increasingly secular society, this would be their contribution to keeping the real meaning of Christmas alive.

Remembering this scene sets us to thinking. Putting Christmas icons on a lawn in front of a spectacularly lit home drew the attention of multitudes. How might we light the inner life of Christian homes to catch the attention of onlookers and showcase the good news about Jesus?

Just as the shimmering crèche created a powerful attraction on the lawn outside, so it is the joy of Bethlehem that will make the household inside attractive as well. Luke's Gospel tells how that joy came to our hearts. It first came to earth that holy night when heaven drew near with incredible news: " 'I bring you good news of great joy that will be for all the people,' " an angel announced to shepherds. " 'Today in the town of David a Savior has been born to you; he is Christ the Lord' " (Luke 2:10, 11). Then, the shepherds' eyes were opened to a skyful of angels singing: " 'Glory to God in the highest, and on earth peace to men on whom his favor rests' " (Luke 2:14).

On that star-spangled night, heaven emptied itself in the grandest of all Christmas gifts—God Himself wrapped in swaddling clothes. The meaning of it all would unfold in the life, death, and resurrection of this Baby named Jesus. But that night the angel choirs couldn't be silenced. For a ragged band of shepherds struck dumb with awe, the angels struck a note higher and broke into breathtaking harmony. In praise of God Incarnate, they set the Bethlehem hillsides alive with music. It was heaven's first press release, the gospel in a nutshell: God's favor has replaced divine wrath against sinful humanity! God and humankind have been brought together in the person of "Christ the Lord"! In Him there is peace on earth and joy for *all* people! Glory to God in the highest, and on earth peace to *humankind* on whom His favor rests.

Too often religion brings only conditional good news, telling people that they can obtain God's favor only if they make sufficient effort. Such a message engenders anxiety as well as joy. But the angels' gospel unequivocally declares that God's own act in sending the Savior to be born in Bethlehem has accomplished whatever needed to be done to bring earth and heaven together again—to restore the divine favor upon all humankind. For religion-burdened souls, for the weary and heavy-laden, these tidings are almost beyond belief. For all who grasp how good the news really is, the sheer joy of it jump-starts faltering spirits better than resuscitator paddles stimulate flagging hearts.

Watch the reaction of the shepherds. "Let's go!" they said. " 'Let's go to Bethlehem and see this thing that has happened, which the Lord has told us about' " (Luke 2:15). They went. And just as the angel said, they found Mary and Joseph and the Baby. And "when they had seen him, they spread the word concerning what had been told them about this child" (Luke 2:17). There's no way people who catch wind of this news can keep it to themselves!

Spreading the joy nearby

We simply can't contain good news. Our eyes light up. Our hearts race. Sometimes we stumble over words as we try to get the details out. We want to share it first with those near and dear to us. Like when Ron and I got engaged.

Ron had proposed on a moonlit Saturday night by a lake, and I'd said, "Yes." When I came home, my parents were still awake. I was so ecstatic, I could hardly get to my room without telling them, but we had decided that we would tell them together. It was Tuesday before the four of us were all present at once, and by then we thought we would burst. That evening when Ron was present, we summoned my parents to the living room. We could both practically hear our hearts pounding.

I could see a little smile lurking at the corners of my mother's mouth, and I suspected she knew what was coming. My dad just had this puzzled look on his face. But then the words came tumbling out: "We want to get married. . . . We hope that's OK with you. . . . Ron has a call to ministry. . . . We'll be staying here in Berrien Springs while he goes to seminary." Mom just beamed. Then Dad, caught off guard at first, began to grin—a face-engulfing grin that conveyed the much-sought-after approval. From that moment, the news went out, and they joined us in the spreading!

"Our work for Christ is to begin with the family, in the home. . . . There is no missionary field more important than this," counseled Ellen White.[1] John's account of the experience of Andrew, a disciple of John the Baptist, captures the excitement of sharing Jesus with family. On two occasions when the Baptist and Jesus were together, Andrew had heard his master call Jesus "the Lamb of God" (John 1:29, 36). This so impressed him that he and a friend spent a day with Jesus.

That day with Jesus convinced Andrew that Jesus was the Messiah. By nightfall, he couldn't contain his joy. The Bible says, "The first thing Andrew did was to find his brother Simon [Peter] and tell him, 'We have found the Messiah' " (John 1:41). Andrew apparently gave such an enthusiastic report that he caught his brother's attention. But Andrew wasn't content merely to report; he became a connector—he arranged for Peter to meet the Master. After making introductions, however, Andrew stepped back. From there on, Jesus and Peter would develop a relationship unique to themselves. Here we have a simple formula for sharing the gospel: *An enthusiastic personal report about Jesus* plus *an introduction to Him as a person.*

The hearts of children are fertile soil for sowing gospel seed. Recently, our friends Glenn and Emmi made our day by sending us photos of their eighteen-month-old daughter Selene in her Sabbath School. Jesus' birth was the program theme. Against a backdrop of a flannel board on which felt angels hovered at all angles just as the little people had deposited them, Selene was taking her turn at holding the Baby Jesus, ready to place Him on the hay in the tiny manger. We couldn't help but reflect on how important the love of family and friends, the involvement of her parents with her at home and in Sabbath School, and the support of faithful children's leaders are to her early spiritual development.

Sometimes parents mistakenly assume that as children grow, they will simply absorb the family's faith. While children and young people do learn by observation, they need learning experiences tailored just for them and a personal introduction to Jesus. Deuteronomy 6 is insistent on this point: The best religious education grows out of connectedness with our children in daily life. Time for both planned and spontaneous worship and spiritual sharing between parents and their young will greatly increase the likelihood that the next generation will also become people of faith.

The Bible is optimistic about the influence of a Christian on a nonbelieving spouse. In Bible times, new converts wondered whether staying married to an unbelieving spouse might be offensive to God or bring defilement upon themselves and their children. The apostle Paul quieted their fears, assuring them that the sacred state of marriage and its intimacies are to continue even though only one spouse professes faith in Christ. The Christian partner "sanctifies" the other and the couple's children, he says—not in the sense of encroaching on their freedom to choose to accept or reject all that Christ has accomplished for them, but because the believer brings them into contact with the blessings of God's grace (see 1 Corinthians 7:13, 14).

God clearly prefers that such marriages be kept intact. A stable family life benefits both the spouses and their children. If the non-Christian spouse chooses to stay in the marriage, the loving kindness, unwavering fidelity, humble service, and winsome witness of the believer create the best likelihood of winning that spouse to Christ. However, God doesn't require believers to put their safety and well-being or that of their children at risk at the hands of an abusive spouse in order to bring salvation. Neither does the biblical concept of submission in marriage require such sacrifice.

The matter of submission raises another corollary point. The biblical principle is that submission in Christian marriage is mutual and voluntary—out of reverence for Christ and after His example of love for the church (see Ephesians 5:21, 25). When a believer applies the principle of Christian submission to his or her marital relationship to an unbelieving partner, the believer's first allegiance is always to Christ.

Of course, an unbelieving partner may decide to abandon the marriage. The ending of a marriage is almost always attended by great trauma, but the merciful word of our God—who upholds human freedom of choice—is "let him do so." The believer "is not bound in such circumstances" (1 Corinthians 7:15). Such families will, however, need a lot of caring and practical support as they grieve the loss of once-meaningful relationships and find healing and new beginnings.

Taking joy to the world

To catch the joy of the gospel is to contract a beneficial joy virus. Infected people are highly contagious. They spread their "disease" everywhere they go. The book of Acts records the ripple effect outward from Jerusalem, where the early church had set up headquarters: "Those who had been scattered preached the word wherever they went" (Acts 8:4).

In Philippi, the message came to a prison warden and his family. It happened the night after Paul and Silas were imprisoned after an encounter with merchants whose wallets were threatened by the evangelists' ministry. The evangelists went right on ministering in the jail, praying and singing among fellow inmates. When a surreal earthquake suddenly sprang open the doors of this lockup at midnight and unfettered the prisoners, the jailer, fearing the prisoners had escaped, was about to commit suicide. But Paul called out in time to stop him, assuring him that no one had escaped. The deeply stirred warden, having heard earlier the praying and singing of these unusual prisoner-preachers, cried out, "Sirs, what must I do to be saved?"

"Believe in the Lord Jesus, and you will be saved—you and your household," they told him. "Then they spoke the word of the Lord to him and to all the others in his house. . . . Immediately he and all his family were baptized. . . . And the whole family was filled with joy, because they had come to believe in God" (Acts 16:31–34, Thompson NIV).

Sharing by proclamation. The jailer and his family caught the joy virus through proclamation—the direct declaration of the Christian message. Paul consistently proclaimed the gospel in his letters using clear discourse and imagery that can bring understanding as certainly today as in Bible times. Paul explained the gospel by comparing and contrasting the two "Adams" and their families—the "first man Adam" of Genesis and Christ, the "last Adam" (1 Corinthians 15:45). The Bible says families are so tightly connected that the sin of Adam, as the first member of the human family, brought condemnation and death upon the entire race (Romans 5:12–21; 1 Corinthians 15:52).

However, God, in His great love for humankind, united His Son to the human race through incarnation to be the Second, or "last,"

Adam. The good news of the gospel is that "in Christ all will be made alive" (1 Corinthians 15:22). Just as the human race was in Adam, the human race is now, by God's own doing, in Christ (see, e.g., 1 Corinthians 1:30; Ephesians 1:3; Galatians 3:28). Just as in Adam, we bear the consequences of his unrighteousness, so in Christ, we reap the benefits and blessings of His righteousness (Romans 5:12–21). This is the good news of the gospel.

God has given humankind a choice. He won't force on anyone the benefits of all that Christ has accomplished for us. Because God values human freedom, either people can reject what He has made them to be in His Son or they can accept it. Scripture calls the positive response a variety of things—believing (1 Timothy 4:10), receiving God's abundant grace and of the gift of righteousness (Romans 5:17), considering oneself "dead to sin but alive to God in Christ Jesus" (Romans 6:11), and so forth. As was true of the Philippian jailor and his household, baptism signifies our acceptance of redeemed status in Christ and personally seals our identity with the last Adam (see Romans 6:4).

Sharing by modeling. Alongside *proclamation,* the Bible instruction to "follow" (KJV) or "imitate" (NIV) Christian leadership spotlights *modeling* as another important way people share the message of Christ. "Consider the outcome of their [your leaders'] way of life and imitate their faith" (Hebrews 13:7). Paul urged his followers, "Imitate me" (1 Corinthians 4:16). With proclamation, faith springs up in the heart through hearing (see Romans 10:17). With modeling, faith is born through seeing. People tend to become like whomever or whatever they watch (see Ephesians 5:1; 1 Thessalonians 1:6; Hebrews 6:12; 3 John 1:11). Usually, making disciples involves some combination of both proclamation and modeling.

Relational modeling is especially valuable in the induction of believers into the lifestyle of faith. It applies particularly in settings such as the home, where imitation is common. Children imitate their parents and siblings; married partners often find themselves doing as their partners do. Through the living out of their faith, couples and families can bear Christian witness to other couples and families. All human examples of faith are flawed, of course, but the scriptural call is for individuals to follow believers who follow Christ.

People can grasp the gospel as they see its fruits demonstrated in the lives of others like themselves. "Social influence," wrote Ellen White, "is a wonderful power. We can use it if we will as a means of helping those about us."[2]

Ron's uncle Dorrance loved company. "The door is always open," he'd say, and everyone knew he meant his heart as well. Ron and his cohorts fondly reminisce about the church socials at his uncle's home and the midwinter ice-skating parties on the rink he made of his front yard. Uncle Dorrance had a Phillips reel-to-reel tape recorder, a first in their farming community. He enjoyed recording kids' voices and introducing the kids to themselves.

On one occasion, Uncle Dorrance gathered the kids around the dinner table and poured out some metal filings and a few small nails on the tabletop. The children grew wide-eyed as the filings and nails jumped to attention like miniature soldiers and started marching in formation around the table. How did they do that? It was magic, he said, keeping them in suspense as long as possible. Then he pulled a magnet out from under the table. He did his best to explain the theory behind magnets, but mostly he enjoyed seeing the children's eyes light up as they took turns moving it around under the table, enthralled by its incredible pulling power.

David Mace explains the profound magnetic influence the homes of Christians can have: "The Christian home is, in fact, by far the most powerful evangelizing agency in the world. Its evangelism, however, is not aggressive; it is persuasive. It proclaims its message not by words, but by deeds. It does not tell others what they *should* be; it shows them what they *could* be. By their gracious influence, Christian homes win more converts than all the preachers put together. Give us enough of them, and the world would soon be a Christian world; for the world's life rises to the higher levels only as its homes do so."[3]

Hospitality

Often mentioned in Scripture and provided by households as different as those of Abraham and Sarah (Genesis 18:1–8) and Zacchaeus (Luke 19:1–9), hospitality reaches out to meet people's basic needs for rest, food, and fellowship. Jesus attached theological significance to such home use when He said that feeding the hungry and giving drink to the thirsty were acts of service done to Him (cp. Matthew 25:34–40). Hospitality may range from these simple offerings to more extended acts, such as lending a room while an abuse victim seeks more permanent living arrangements. It may mean extending a smile and a friendly word, or offering to give a hand to an overextended caregiver, or studying the Bible with a seeker for truth. "Families shaped by Christian faith and strong love for one another can offer an extraordinary gift in welcoming others into their homes. As they live their lives in front of their guests, faithful though flawed Christians can model practices within a healthy family, warts and all. Such welcome provides a context for a very natural, low-key yet powerful form of mentoring."[4]

In *Christian Witness in a Postmodern World,* Harry Lee Poe assesses the emerging culture of postmodernism. Within a highly mobile society in which traditional family life has broken down, he says, relationships are a prized commodity, for they are difficult to obtain and maintain. "The postmodern age," he concludes, "is an anonymous age with a yearning for relationship."[5] Poe believes this is a golden hour for Christianity because of the message at its heart: a personal God has reconciled humankind to Himself and to each other in Christ. "The postmodern generation will not visit the church building. They will not go to the lecture. They will not join the organization. The church looks like just one more institution. They are interested not in institutions but in relationships. . . . For them to listen to us, the sharing of the gospel has to take place in a relational way, that is, a conversation."[6] This is what David and Vera Mace had in mind when they wrote, "A Christian home should be . . . a center of contagious friendliness, with open doors toward all human need."[7]

In a world waiting for relationship, Christians' homes are in a strategic position to spread the news of a relational God and of the *koinōnia* of His redeemed community. Wonderful are the possibilities ahead for hearts and homes that have become contagious with joy!

---

1. Ellen G. White, *The Adventist Home* (Hagerstown, Md.: Review and Herald, 1952), 35.

2. Ellen G. White, *The Ministry of Healing* (Nampa, Idaho: Pacific Press®, 1942), 354.

3. David and Vera Mace, *In the Presence of God: Readings for Christian Marriage* (Philadelphia, Penn.: The Westminster Press, 1985), 113.

4. Christine D. Pohl and Pamela J. Buck, "Hospitality and Family Life," *Family Ministry,* Fall 2004, 16.

5. Harry Lee Poe, *Christian Witness in a Postmodern World* (Nashville, Tenn.: Abingdon Press, 2001), 27.

6. Ibid., 34.

7. Mace and Mace, 98.

Turning Time

A few years ago, we crossed the Allenby Bridge over the Jordan River between Jordan and Israel. This famous international link between Amman and Jerusalem, closed during years of Arab-Israeli conflict, had been reopened only a matter of days earlier. In the oppressive heat, the only green shrubs clung for survival along the banks of the shallow, narrow rivulet that comprises the Jordan just upstream from the Dead Sea. The arid, sub-sea-level landscape has likely remained the same for two millennia.

That day our minds wandered back through history-laden time, imagining the unorthodox prophet John ben Zechariah stirring up a spiritual tempest by these murky waters. With thunderous preaching, a radical message, and camel's hair garb, this cousin of Jesus must have cut a striking figure that drew both the serious and the inquisitive to his Jordan baptistry. Our excitement stemmed from something more than our mere presence in this home territory of the Baptist, however. For some years now, we had felt a curious point of contact with the Jordan prophet.

In John's time, Messianic expectation ran high that soon the land of Judea would be freed of its Roman subjugation. Hearing of the unconventional desert phenomenon, a contingent of Jewish religious leaders was sent down from Jerusalem to check him out. Who was he, really? Could he be the Messiah?

When they learned from his own lips that he was not, they followed up with another query. Their second question stemmed from a belief popular among many Jewish teachers of the law—that the prophet Elijah would appear as the forerunner of the Messiah (see Matthew 17:10; Mark 6:15). "Are you Elijah?" they asked (John 1:21).

John's answer to their inquiry was again, "I am not" (John 1:21). Later, however, after the Baptist's horrible death by Herod's drunken decree, Jesus would eulogize him, saying, "I tell you, Elijah has already come, and they did not recognize him." Scripture continues, "Then the disciples understood that he was talking to them about John the Baptist" (Matthew 17:12, 13). The linking of John the Baptist with the Old Testament prophecy of Elijah's coming was our touch point with this desert place and its history.

Recalling Elijah

The Jewish tradition regarding the personal appearance of Elijah just before the coming of Messiah had its origin in the final verses of the Old Testament canon—in a cryptic announcement made at the close of the book of Malachi: " 'I will send you the prophet Elijah before that great and dreadful day of the LORD comes. He will turn the hearts of the fathers to their children, and the hearts of the children to their fathers; or else I will come and strike the land with a curse' " (Malachi 4:5, 6). The reference to turning "the hearts of the fathers to their children and the hearts of the children to their fathers" especially in the period "before that great and dreadful day of the Lord" has made this a verse worthy of our best efforts to discover its meaning for families. The trail of this text winds through both Testaments, beginning with its message to the original hearers.

Malachi was attempting to get the Judeans to turn their hearts toward God rather than to persist in a half-hearted, inconsistent, institutionalized religion. Though some in the land were spiritually sensitive to Jehovah (Malachi 3:16), most were pseudoreligious. Like the crew aboard the *Titanic,* the Judeans felt smug in their accomplishments, and their religion reflected a pernicious self-sufficiency. The leaders were moving at full throttle toward creating a powerful religious state. They were totally in denial regarding their true condition and the dangers it posed. Their responses to the prophet show that not for one minute did they slow to reflect seriously on his forthright assessment of their spiritual condition, let alone consider changing their course. Listening to even a few examples of the divine appeals and Judah's rejoinders reminds one of a parent going one-on-one with a headstrong adolescent. Note the tones of feeling in these bits of the exchange:

Father (desperate and exasperated): " 'I have loved you' " (Malachi 1:2). Accent the "loved." We're hearing the voice of a loving parent spurned. "But I loved you. . . . How could you . . . ?"

Judah (cocky and unconvinced): " ' "How have you loved us?" ' " (verse 2). Accent the "how," as in, "Yeah? How? Just how have You loved us? What have You done for us lately?"

Father: " 'A son honors his father . . . [but] you show contempt for my name' " (verse 6).

Judah: " ' "How have we shown contempt for your name?" ' " (verse 6).

Father: " 'You place defiled food on my altar' " (verse 7).

Judah: " ' "How have we defiled you?" ' " (verse 7) "How does the food we place on our altar defile *You* or show contempt for *Your* name?"

Father: " 'Return to me, and I will return to you' " (Malachi 3:7). The appeal comes straight from the heart of God—not in the sense of "If first you return, then I'll return," but "Let's get together. Just come back to Me. I'm here, ready and waiting."

Judah (resistant): " ' "How are we to return?" ' " (verse 7). Read between the lines: "What do You mean 'return'? We've not turned from You; You're the One who's turned away from us."

As in every time and place, there were, thank God, responsive people who talked Malachi's message over with one another and committed themselves to the fear of the Lord and to honoring His name (see Malachi 3:16). But beyond the few, the appeal for a turnaround in Judah was fruitless. Centuries later, Jesus would comment on a similar situation in His day, " 'These people honor me with their lips, but their hearts are far from me' " (Matthew 15:8).

Before the frustrated prophet Malachi finishes, before Scripture lapses into a four-century silence, Malachi announces that God will give His people one more opportunity to turn around. He will send the greatest of all spiritual reformers as His mouthpiece. In all the history of Israel, one moment stands out as the high-water mark of heart-turning. During the awful period of spiritual drought and disaster when Baal worship nearly obliterated Jehovah worship altogether, the prophet Elijah had almost single-handedly brought reconciliation between God and His people. Like a biblical version of an Abraham Lincoln, a Mahatma Gandhi, a Winston Churchill, Elijah was synonymous with a critical period in his nation's history. God will send that man, said Malachi, and he *will* turn hearts. Count on it.

Prophet of turning

Elijah's central role in the divine-human drama that unfolded on Mount Carmel forever marked him as the legendary prophet of heart-turning. To understand fully the prophecy of his reappearance, we must understand what really happened on the mountain.

The introduction of Baal worship in Israel by Jezebel, the Sidonian wife of King Ahab, propelled the nation into an unprecedented period of moral decay and down-with-Jehovah sentiment. The Tishbite prophet Elijah ("Jehovah-is-my-God") stepped onto the scene and, over a three-year period, single-handedly faced down the imposter religion and reestablished the worship of the true God. The mountaintop confrontation between Elijah and the heathen priests capped the anti-Baal campaign (1 Kings 18).

Atop Mount Carmel, Elijah set the spiritual table for the people with two options on the menu: " 'If the LORD is God, follow him; but if Baal is God, follow him' " (verse 21). To enable the Israelites to decide which god was worthy of their allegiance, he proposed that each side prepare an animal for sacrifice. " 'Then,' " said he, " 'you call on the name of your god, and I will call on the name of the LORD. The god who answers by fire—he is God' " (verse 24). No approval to this plan was forthcoming from the opposing priests, but the people—Elijah's primary interest—said, " 'What you say is good' " (verse 24).

The Baalites tried all day, but their incantations failed to set their sacrifice afire. Then Elijah stood to his feet, deliberately drawing attention to God's redemptive plan by calling the people together at the time of the evening sacrifice. God had specified that at this hour, Israel was to offer a sacrifice daily (see Exodus 29:41), signifying "their constant dependence upon the atoning blood of Christ."[1] The invitation that Elijah extended, "Come here to me," foreshadowed the coming of One who would befriend sinners and draw them close to Himself (see Luke 15:1). No less does He love our wayward children. Patiently He follows their journeys, again and again intersecting their paths with gestures of love and grace, His arms always ready for embrace.

Elijah painstakingly rebuilt the broken-down altar to Jehovah, recounting as he piled stone on stone the nation's covenant history with God. Altar-building continues in families each time we uplift Jesus and His sacrifice, whether in planned or spontaneous times of worship and spiritual reflection.

When the altar and sacrifice were in place just as God had commanded, Elijah raised his voice in prayer: " 'Answer me, O LORD, answer me, so these people will know that you, O LORD, are God, and that you are turning their hearts back again' " (verse 37). Fear and anxiety were in the air. God had been clear about His wrath against sin. So Elijah began by asking God for evidence that He had turned His fatherly heart toward His people and is reconciled to them. In so praying, the prophet echoed the prayers of spiritual leaders throughout Israel's history that God might turn His face once again toward His erring children: "Return to us, O God Almighty!" "Restore us again, O God our Savior, and put away your displeasure toward us" (Psalms 80:14; 85:4).

Elijah had no doubt where God's heart was in all of this. Sin is real, and so is sinful humanity's separation from a holy God. But sin—even the ugliness and degradation of Baal worship—doesn't catch God by surprise. In His Lamb, "slain from the creation of the world" (Revelation 13:8), He has made a way for the cosmic cleft to be closed. Satan would hide that truth. His intent, coupled with the degenerative effects of sin on human nature, engenders doubt regarding God's love and willingness to take sinners back to Himself. Without assurance of God's love and His divine favor, the heart faints; with such assurance, it springs to life with praise and thanksgiving. Elijah's prayer seeks the revival that only the knowledge of God's reconciling grace in Christ can bring.

Elijah's prayer also recognizes that it is God alone who reconciles sinners to Himself. It is He who turns their hearts back again and draws them to Himself. We cannot turn our hearts to God; we can only unclasp our hands to receive His grace—and that, He freely gives. Note the words of Jeremiah: " ' "Restore me, and I will return, because you are the LORD my God" ' "; "Restore us to yourself, O LORD, that we may return" (Jeremiah 31:18; Lamentations 5:21).

What followed was a divine act, as Heavenly Father gave mighty evidence of His own turning and the restoration of His people to His heart. The destroying fire fell not upon the guilty, who deserved to die, but upon the Sacrifice. In one mighty demonstration of grace, their eyes—and ours—were turned upon Jesus, who would be made "sin for us, that in him we might become the righteousness of God" (2 Corinthians 5:21). In an instant, gone were the animal, the wood, the water, and the stones. Even the dust of the earth was licked up in a grand display of omnipotent grace. Confession and praise burst from the people's lips, " 'The LORD—he is God! The LORD—he is God!' " (1 Kings 18:39).

The false priests, unrepentant and resistant to the end, were executed. Then the rains came. Refreshing rain, the likes of which had not been seen in more than three years, while Elijah was doing combat with Baal, the Canaanite rain god. Now the drought that cursed the land was lifted, and everyone who felt its restorative power knew for sure it was Jehovah and not Baal who sent the rain.

While the work of the first Elijah was to bring news of Heavenly Father's heart-turning that His Israelite children might return to Him, the prophet's ministry surely has its application for families of all time. Many families feel distance, even estrangement, in relationships, but have no model for heart-turning. Sometimes there are cultural barriers to marriage partners or parents and children becoming open and vulnerable in their relationships.

Once, when our boys were just about school age, we promised to lead a weekend retreat for pastoral families in West Virginia. It was to be a family affair, and we all looked forward to it. On the trip from Washington, D.C., however, West Virginia threw us curves—quite literally. I (Ron) badly underestimated the driving time. Since "late" is not in my vocabulary, I careened over hills, straightening curves as we went, tossing the boys about in the back of our station wagon, where they were playing. Repeatedly, they poked their heads through the curtain of clothes on the metal clothes rod that stretched across the middle of our car to ask, "Are we there yet?" The annoying grating of metal on metal compounded the frustration I felt. Eventually, when the boys asked the question again, I braked hard and stopped. I'm not at all proud now to remember how I vented my frustration on my family. Then, shocking everyone, I turned the car around and headed home. "We can't go there and talk about family," I said. "We can't even keep our own family together in the car."

Karen tried to calm me, but my knuckles just grew whiter on the steering wheel, my gaze more intent on the homeward road. Precious minutes and miles passed. At last, something she said broke through. "You need to stop and talk to the boys," she said. "Let's just pull over here."

I stopped the car. Knowing that I was wrong, and fumbling for words, I apologized—something I had never before done as a dad. After I asked the boys' forgiveness, they hugged my neck and I experienced grace. We stretched our legs doing quick laps in the grass, and Karen took my hand as we walked back to the car. When we turned once more toward the retreat center, we knew we had something to share. Our family will always link heart-turning with that grassy spot near the Virginia–West Virginia state line.

The Elijah message beyond Elijah

When interviewed at the Jordan, John did not personally identify himself with Elijah. Yet, in what seems to be a clear reference to the Malachi prophecy, the angel Gabriel had said to Zechariah, his father, "Many of the people of Israel will he bring back to the Lord their God. And he will go on before the Lord, in the spirit and power of Elijah, to turn the hearts of the fathers to their children and the disobedient to the wisdom of the righteous—to make ready a people prepared for the Lord" (Luke 1:16, 17). Perhaps in the centuries since Malachi, the apocalyptic myth had been blown up to such proportions that the Baptist could not identify with the religious leaders' expectations. Perhaps he was just content to remain a " 'voice . . . calling in the desert, "Make straight the way of the Lord" ' " (John 1:23).

Jesus posthumously awarded John this identification with Elijah because He discerned that John indeed fulfilled the deeper meaning of the prophecy. Jesus knew that the issues of the nations—of Israel in Elijah's day, of Judah in Malachi's day, and of Judea in His own and John's day—were of a piece. Religious leaders and their followers were smug in their religious ways, but without living faith and in denial of their true spiritual condition. Like a farmer who plows hard ground to prepare it to receive seed, John denounced sin and urged sinners to repent. His message connected in people's minds the reality of their sinful condition and their need for a Savior. By exposing the shallow, self-centered hypocrisy of those who claimed Abraham as their father, he sought to open the deeper meaning of connection with God as Father.

Most importantly, Jesus pointed to John as "the Elijah who was to come" (Matthew 11:14) because He knew that Malachi's expression, the "day of the LORD" (Malachi 4:5), meant Elijah's arrival was to coincide with His own coming into the world to seek and save the lost. Beyond the call for repentance, the Elijah who was to come would identify the One who saves and would introduce Him to a waiting world. And John had been Jesus' herald, the first to introduce Him as "the Lamb of God, who takes away the sin of the world!" (John 1:29, 36). By directing his own disciples and his hearers to Jesus, John truly turned "many of the people of Israel . . . back to the Lord their God."

So, John the Baptist was the voice of Elijah heralding the great day of the Lord as Christ completed the suffering-servant phase of His work. Today, as time marches toward that great Day of the Lord when Jesus will come as King of kings, people with Elijah voices have again stepped onto the stage to trumpet the gospel of grace to the world with renewed urgency. Through every means of communication available, the incomparable news rings clear: God has turned human hearts back to Him again, and He appeals to each one to accept His gracious gift and be turned toward Him. Paul calls all Christians to this ministry of reconciliation—as always, in response to what God has already done for us in Christ: "God was reconciling the world to himself in Christ, not counting men's sins against them. And he has committed to us the message of reconciliation. We are therefore Christ's ambassadors, as though God were making his appeal through us. We implore you on Christ's behalf: Be reconciled to God" (2 Corinthians 5:19, 20).

In Jesus' parable of the prodigal son, He who came to reveal the heart of Heavenly Father pours into a family story the essence of the human story. In its narrative detail, it mirrors the Elijah prophecy, for it too is about the turning of hearts—fathers to children and children to fathers. The critical points on which the parable turns are, in fact, the moments at which the hearts of a son and his father are revealed.

At some point in the downward spiral of the out-of-control life of this profligate son, his heart turned toward his father. Famished, filthy, lonely, and desperate, the son, Jesus said, "came to himself." Maybe in that instant his mind was able somehow to surmount the assault of present living conditions as sweet images of home flooded his being. But his flights of fancy were short-lived.

No, of course he couldn't go back. He had no stake in "home" anymore. What he'd done was tantamount to killing his father. But his father's face . . . something in his father's face as he'd closed the gate behind himself had etched its way into his memory. Remembering it allowed him to begin crafting his speech. "Father, I have sinned against heaven and against you. I am no longer worthy to be called your son; make me like one of your hired men." He'd be a servant, but he'd be home!

Every day the father had gone to the gate to watch. Every day he had relived the parting, his eyes burning again with every recollection. Every day he found himself looking up the lane, his heart quickening whenever he saw someone coming in the distance. If only, if only, he could contact his boy. He would tell him that he'd forgiven everything. Nothing more had to be done but for him to come home. A son is a son forever; nothing can change that except the son's own persistent, deliberate choice.

But wait, he knows that gait!

And then both of them are running, running, running. At first the son hesitates, but then he gives himself over to love and to his father's embrace. He starts his speech, but his father stops him before he can get to the part about being a hired servant. "My son who was lost is found! Let the party begin!" the father hollers to the hills. And then he starts giving orders to everyone.

Father God too waits at the gate, His heart turned toward His children, His eyes looking eagerly up the lane. The party is prepared. All that remains is for His sons and daughters to turn their hearts toward Him and come home.

---

1. Ellen G. White, *Patriarchs and Prophets* (Nampa, Idaho: Pacific Press®, 1958), 352.

Appendix: Chiastic Structure of the Song of Solomon*

Song 1:2–2:2

(A)   Wife's desire for her husband (1:2)   (A)
Solomon named (1:5)
"My own vineyard" (1:6)
Silver (1:11)
"My breasts" (1:13)
Evaluation of her (favorable) (1:15, 16)
Cedar (1:17)

Song 2:3–17

(B)   The apple tree (2:3–5)   (B)
Charge to the Jerusalem girls (2:6, 7)
The beloved visits her home (2:8, 9)
His invitation to an outing (2:10–15)
Marriage covenant formula (2:16)

Song 3:1–4:15

(C)   Dream I, search-encounter (3:1–4)   (C)
Charge to the Jerusalem girls (3:5)
Praise of Solomon's procession (3:6–10)
Wedding scene (3:11)
Praise of bride's beauty (4:1–7)
Praise of bride's character (4:8–15)

Song 4:16

(D)   Her invitation (4:16)   (D)

Song 5:1

(D′)   His response (5:1)   (D′)

Song 5:2–7:9

(C′)   Dream II, encounter-search (5:2–7)   (C′)
Charge to the Jerusalem girls (5:8)
Praise of Solomon's person (5:9–6:3)
Praise of bride's character (6:4–10)
Dance of Mahanaim (6:11–13)
Praise of bride's beauty (7:1–9)

Song 7:10–8:5

(B′)   Marriage covenant formula (7:10)   (B′)
Her invitation to an outing (7:11–13)
A wish that he might visit her home (8:1, 2)
Charge to the Jerusalem girls (8:3, 4)
The apple tree (8:5)

Song 8:6–14

Cedar (8:8, 9)

(A′)   Evaluation of her (unfavorable) (8:8, 9)   (A′)
"My breasts" (8:10)
Silver (8:11)
"My own vineyard" (8:12)
Solomon named (8:12)
Wife's desire for her husband (8:14)

L - 517 - 200 - 8136

Shama - 517 - 200 - 8135

---

*Adapted from William H. Shea, "The Chiastic Structure of the Song of Songs," *Zeitschrift für die Alttestamentliche Wissenschaft,* 1980, 92. Note: Variations within the chiasm exist. The overall order of segments in C′, for example, is not the reverse of C, as is the case with the other segments.